Humanus Astrologicus

Astrological reasons in rhyme
why we do what we do

Deborah Smith Parker

Humanus Astrologicus

**Astrological reasons in rhyme
why we do what we do**

Deborah Smith Parker

Astrologicus Press

ISBN 10: 0-981-4787-0-0
ISBN 13: 978-0-9814787-0-8

Second Edition

Cover artwork, Donald G. Phillips.
Cover design, interior design and typography, Teri Rider.

Library of Congress Control Number: 2008901698

Astrologicus Press
San Diego, California
www.astrologicuspress.com

Printed in USA

00 19 18 17 16 15   3 4 5 6 7 8 9

DEDICATION

In loving memory of my parents who showed me in so many ways the power and magic behind the stars.

FIRST MAGIC

Stories, their magic first drawn
in my imagination
by the voices of my parents.

My mother's voice
flowed under me,
gently bubbling water
tumbling from the pages
of many wondrous books,
and I would float all warm
in her circling currents.

My father's voice
stole thunder from the heavens
to tell of times when gods
first climbed down from the stars
to meet us on the same field of battle,
and forever woke those gods
who slept inside of me.

Deborah Smith Parker

TABLE OF CONTENTS

ACKNOWLEDGMENTS

Many thanks go to my friends and colleagues from the San Diego Astrological Society for their support and enthusiasm for this book project. I'm particularly grateful to Jim Hennum, Claire-France Perez, Mavis Mathews, and Anne Beversdorf for their helpful and tireless feedback on the astrological content of the verses in this book.

I'm grateful to my non-astrological friends and associates for their willingness to be my "lab rats" in testing out the material in this book in informal focus groups.

Thanks to Claudia Black, Sandy Foote, Ted Holt, and Karen Hawthorne for their reviews of the manuscript, and to Melissa Pregill for her edits—and for her valiant and sometimes successful attempts to temper my tendency to write in long, compound-complex sentences drilled into me by the Wisconsin school system, particularly my professors and instructors from the English Department at the University of Wisconsin-Madison.

I'm grateful to Teri Rider who managed the production end of this book, prodded me when I needed it and became a good friend in the process.

Thanks to Don Phillips for his inspired painting, "Amongst the Stars," for the cover art.

I'd like to thank my father-in-law, Ray Parker, for his suggestions drawn from his many years as a Hollywood writer and who was the first to suggest that my astrological poetry could become a book.

I want to express my deep gratitude to my husband, Jeff, for understanding the importance of this book to me and for supporting me in his many surprising and wondrous Aquarian ways.

PREFACE

In my over 30 years as an astrologer I've observed there are many reasons that people are attracted to astrology. They want to know the unknown. They're looking for relief from a troublesome repeating pattern. They seek validation for who they are. Sometimes they're just plain fascinated by the subject. Whatever the reason, when they begin to read about astrology they are often overwhelmed by its complex and foreign terminology. Most astrological books are written for the few who will become astrological students, not the majority who are merely curious. However, anyone can enjoy and understand astrology's message for them in *Humanus Astrologicus*.

Humanus Astrologicus not only speaks directly to you about who you are and what you do, it also guarantees you many laughs. It takes the complexity out of astrological books by presenting your astrological characteristics with humor that doesn't sacrifice accuracy. And it does so through poetic verse. Now stay with me here! This isn't poetry dense with arcane symbolism and obscure allusions forced on us by teachers who wanted us to identify a rigidly prescribed interpretation. *Humanus Astrologicus* is easy to understand and you get to decide how it applies to you.

Astrological books are written in prose which is the narrative form we normally speak and write in. Prose is accurate but not as memorable as poetry. For instance, a standard astrological book would describe those born with the Sun in the sign of Virgo (what it means when someone says, "I'm a Virgo") as efficient, analytical and detail oriented. They color inside the lines and cross all the t's. They want to be helpful and like being busy. That's accurate but not memorable. Here's how *Humanus Astrologicus* describes it.

> *If things don't work they want to change them.*
> *They'll be glad to rearrange them*
> *And can, incidentally,*
> *Show you how to incrementally.*
> *If a project is well analyzed,*
> *The budget's not been compromised,*
> *One may assume that, ergo,*
> *It is managed by a Virgo.*

Another example: One of the first things any description of Sun in Libra will tell you is that Libras must weigh the elements of every decision, and that they have to vocalize their process. Here's how *Humanus Astrologicus* says that:

> *Oh, I could really tell some tales*
> *Of Libras balancing their scales,*
> *Like if they say, "Let's see a show,"*
> *Don't grab your coat and start to go*
> *Because they must evaluate*
> *Many times and then restate*
> *The reasons they would like to go*
> *But also why they shouldn't though.*

I learned the power of poetry before I could read and write. Many times I sneaked out of bed to hide on the upstairs landing, peeking through the banister to watch and listen to the party downstairs where my father had been requested again to recite one of the many enthralling story poems he was known for. Men and women in fine evening wear, some seated on the floor, the women with the skirts of their gowns spread out around them, were as focused on my dad as a group of first graders listening to their favorite story.

Poetry is natural to all human beings because its expression is one of images which are our minds' first conceptualizations of how we experience the world. Language is how we articulate those images and communicate them to others. Most of us don't consciously realize that our communication and comprehension depend on constantly translating images into words and words back into images.

The more that language uses images, especially images imbedded in rhythm and rhyme, the more our minds wrap hungrily around them and the easier they lodge in memory. That's why we remember the exact words to songs or verses more easily than we remember standard prose. For example, you can caution someone who has never driven across the American Southwest that it will take longer than a day to drive across Texas. They may or may not remember that in making travel plans. But tell them an old Texas folk saying, *The sun has riz, the sun has set/And we ain't out of Texas yet*, and they won't forget it.

Up until the last few hundred years, the majority of people on this planet were illiterate. It's no accident that they learned principally from the oral traditions of their cultures communicated through song and spoken verse. Some of these are still known today as classical epics, poems, folk music and myths.

Humanus Astrologicus covers more than just Sun signs, which are only the front door to astrology. You have to pass through that door and enter the house to begin to see the real picture of a person emerge through the placements of the other planets. So *Humanus Astrologicus* also provides detailed verses for

Moon, Mercury, Venus, Mars, Jupiter and Saturn in each sign. Most people don't even know they have a Venus or Mercury that would be somewhere, let alone what those planets mean when placed in particular astrological signs. *Humanus Astrologicus* provides the means for you to identify which signs your planets are in so you can know which verses to read that will describe you.

For instance, one of Venus' major roles in astrology is to show us what we want as well as our capacity to attract what we want. Standard astrological fare describes one aspect of Venus in Leo as wanting to be the center of attention and having little problem making that happen. Here's the *Humanus Astrologicus* take on that:

> *As soon as these folks leave the womb*
> *They know how to fill a room.*
> *It doesn't matter where they are,*
> *At work, the gym—they are a star.*
> *They hope their entrances are grand:*
> *"What, no flowers? Where's the band?"*

Another example is Mercury, the chief astrological indicator of how we think and communicate. One aspect of those with Mercury in Pisces, so says a typical astrological description, is that they feel their way through decisions as much or more than they use logic. Here are a few lines demonstrating how *Humanus Astrologicus* describes it:

> *Watching them plot out a course*
> *May make you think they use the Force,*
> *Because they use their intuition*
> *Bringing plans into fruition.*

Both sides of my family contributed to the subject and style of this book. My mother's side gave me a love of literature and my inclination to astrology. Several members of her family—particularly her generation and the one above it—had a quiet tendency to the medial arts that help connect the seen and unseen worlds, including but not limited to astrology. It was rarely talked about since Mom's family's talents in those areas lurked like flounders at the bottom of the family gene pool, buried beneath layers of stalwart Episcopalianism.

My father's side produced those with professorial proficiency in the ancient classics, love for poetry, skill at oratory, and the ability to write. Dad was also an amateur astronomer. He taught my brother and me and many of our friends the constellations of the night sky and how to use each one as a pointer to the next. And he knew all the myths behind the star pictures he introduced us to.

Nothing could stop Dad from planting his telescope in a key spot to view the heavens, not even winter and we lived in Wisconsin, the Land of Perpetual Winter. He would awaken the family at two in the morning to view some astral phenomenon visible from earth only in intervals of decades. After bundling into coats, boots, mittens and scarves, we were then herded to the back yard where we spent most of that time stamping our feet and clapping our mittened hands to keep the circulation going saying, "That's really great, Dad. Can I go inside now?"

I never did see the moons of Jupiter as they moved too rapidly through the telescope for my sleepy eyes to follow. But I always felt deeply the magic of the night sky, the wonder of that enormous spread of stars that serves as both the "ceiling of our world and the floor of the gods" as Dad would say. His stories about the myths associated with the stars connected me to the past in a way nothing else has—to think that hundreds and even thousands of years before people tending their sheep or sailing a night sea looked up in awe at the same starscape I see today. I love to think that parents in those times told their children many of the same stories about the gods and heroes in the star pictures that my father told me.

Dad didn't just recite poetry, he also wrote it and he taught us how. When my brother and I were old enough, many a night would find our family still around the dining room table long after dinner collaborating on some project. In our extended family the "fun" gene was largely recessive, but in our little nucleus it was flamingly dominant. We specialized in humor, especially parody. No subject was safe from us, something I've taken into my writing career today. We cracked ourselves up. People outside the family also thought we were clever. Dad was always writing something for someone, and soon my brother and I slipped into those roles in our worlds.

The seeds for *Humanus Astrologicus* were sown a few years ago when I dusted off a poem I wrote on Sun in Aquarius when I was part of a metaphysical school many years before. The school had a disproportionate number of people with Sun in Aquarius so one year we had a group birthday celebration for them for which I wrote a poem. When I rediscovered it I was already a many times published poet and essayist with more polish than was evident in that work. So I gave the Aquarius poem a complete overhaul, turning it into a much better piece.

I then became inspired to write verses for the eleven other Sun signs with no purpose at the time except to complete the set. Eventually, I followed the natural energy of the solar system and moved from the Sun out to the other planets, writing verses for each planet's placements in each of the twelve signs of the zodiac—and *Humanus Astrologicus* was born.

As this book was in development I conducted informal focus groups with friends and coworkers who knew nothing about astrology. In fact, several were down right skeptical about the value of astrology. However, not only did my lab rats report that the verses fit them, they also said the material made them think about who they are and how they respond to life. My astrological colleagues were surprised not only at the accuracy of the verses, but how they served to put the reader "inside" the meaning of the planetary placements.

Whether you know nothing about astrology or a lot, I hope that in the following pages you will feel the magic of the stars, so dear to me, reaching out to touch you.

THOSE WHOSE GOAL IS TO BE WISE
BEGIN BY OPENING THEIR EYES.
THEN THEIR REWARD THEY'LL SURELY FIND
IS SIGHT FOR WHICH THEY ONCE WERE BLIND.

INTRODUCTION

In a conversation with someone new to astrology, the question invariably comes up, "How can the stars be the cause of who I am and what happens to me?" The 30 second answer is, as the astrologer Zip Dobyns was fond of saying, "The stars do not cause, they indicate."

The longer answer involves my retelling one of the most familiar stories in human history in a way many may find surprising. So get a cup of hot chocolate (or whatever), wrap up in your favorite blankie and settle in. But first a little background on how astrology developed into an integral part of many of the world's cultures, and how the stars became associated with human events and actions.

It is a common misconception that astrology was born in mysticism, delivered through ascetics meditating on lonely mountain tops. It didn't happen that way. Astrology and its root, astronomy, evolved through observation. Our earliest ancestors noticed that the stars formed patterns or pictures that moved through the skies in repeating cycles. They further observed that a few lights in the sky shined with a steadier light than the twinkling light of the stars. These traveled through the star pictures, each at a speed independent of the others and also on predictable schedules.

The star pictures were eventually named constellations and the independently moving lights called planets. The names the ancient Hebrews gave them accurately described their relationship to each other. Their word for constellations was *masloth* meaning highways, and their word for planets was *mazawloth*, meaning wanderers. This was the beginning of the science of astronomy.

The constellations were named for mythic heroes and animals important to survival, linked to the seasons in which they were prominent. For instance, Taurus the bull, known for his fecundity, rules the time of spring planting. Scorpio, the sign of death and eventual rebirth, rules the time after the harvest when plants die. Since astronomy first developed in regions north of the equator, there is quite a northern hemisphere bias to the naming of constellations and the seasons they're associated with.

It was further observed by the ancients that the movements of the planets into different constellations coincided with behaviors and events on earth. They reasoned this could only be the work of gods. Therefore, planets were named for the god associated with the types of events and behaviors a particular planet appeared to evoke, like acts of war with Mars, good fortune with Jupiter, and limitations or losses with Saturn. This was the beginning of astrology. Astronomy and astrology remained linked for a long time until gradually astrology split off as an art but still inseparable from the science of astronomy, a split that remains in culture today.

The earliest civilizations perceived the workings of their worlds largely as chaos. The gods had all the power and humans lived and died subject to their whims. All life activities and events, including human behaviors, were seen as expressions of the moods and desires of the gods, an earlier version of "the devil made me do it." One can only imagine how terrifying that must have been. No wonder the gods played such a dominant role in all ancient cultures. People felt it necessary to establish and maintain rituals, sacrifices and practices that appeased the gods, many of which are evident in the Old Testament.

The foundations for what we know today about astronomy, geometry, life sciences and psychological theory were established by the ancient Greeks, credited as the first to employ the scientific method. They were the first to proclaim that there was order to the universe, that natural laws governed acts of nature, not the gods.

Knowing natural law meant that many phenomena were now predictable. Once the laws became known, so did many of their indicators. Thus, the gods and the stars began to lose some of their power as the perceived cause of events. For instance, the ancient Egyptians originally believed that the yearly appearance of the star Sirius caused the annual flooding of the Nile River. Eventually it became known through science that the annual cycle of rain in that region caused the Nile to flood. Thus, Sirius transitioned from cause to indicator.

The night sky served as calendar and clock for ancient civilizations which were largely agrarian. The phases of the Moon and the rising and setting positions of the constellations became tested indicators of when to prepare the soil, plant crops, and prune and harvest them. Many farmers and gardeners around the globe still rely on these methods in industrialized as well as developing nations.

Astrology emerged as the practice of using the stars as indicators of events and behaviors and in which environments those take place. Astrologers were held in high esteem in ancient cultures. All the kings had them in the regions we now call the Mideast and Mediterranean areas. Astrologers only served the king so the only important environments were those affecting the status of the king and his kingdom. Everyone else lived and died according to the kings' fortunes or lack thereof, including their astrologers. Talk about job pressure! Individuals were insignificant.

Now we come to the story. It is about one of the most historically significant occurrences this planet has ever experienced, and how astrology was an indicator of that occurrence. I'm going to present two perspectives, first as the story was originally recorded two thousand years ago, and second, from an astrologer's viewpoint, because astrology is center stage in this story without getting much credit for its role.

We hear this story in its original form and we retell it every Christmas, about the journey of the very pregnant young couple desperately seeking lodging, the stable the baby was born in, the shepherds, the wise men and especially the star that led everybody to that place. We are surrounded by these images not just in churches but in seasonal merchandising, advertising, decorations and music.

There's only one problem with this story as we retell it—that pesky star. How we tell the story and how the story is originally written don't really jive. The Gospel of Luke is traditionally read at Christmas services all over the world. Children dressed as all the characters (I was a sheep in my first Christmas pageant) parade up church aisles to reenact the tale, always following a star. However, there is no mention of a star in Luke. There is no mention of a star in Mark or John. The only mention of a star is in Matthew. If you read Matthew 2:1-16 carefully you will see that the only ones who appeared to be aware of the star's presence were the wise men.

Here's how it's recorded. The wise men were astrologers. This we know because the Greek word the Gospel writer used to describe them is *magos*, translated as wise men or magi. According to *Strong's Concordance* (an exhaustive cross-reference of every word in the King James Bible back to the word in the original biblical text) *magos* means "the name given by the Babylonians (Chaldeans), Medes, Persians, and others, to the wise men, teachers, priests, physicians, astrologers, seers, interpreters of dreams…." These may sound like discreet "professions" but in the context of the times this is a pretty accurate job description of the duties of an astrologer. These few verses in Matthew are the only ones in the Gospels that use the word *magos* which only applies to the wise men. In any event, they came into Jerusalem following a star that heralded the birth of a king, saying, "We have seen his *star in the east*," (King James Version) or, "We have observed his *star at its rising*" (New Revised Standard Version).

The word indicating the star's presence that both versions interpreted slightly differently is *anatole*, which, according to *Strong's*, means "rising (of the sun and stars)." It is simple physics that heavenly bodies appear to rise in the east due to the rotation of the earth. If non-astrologers say they witnessed a star rising, they more than likely are describing watching it physically rise in the night sky. Astrologers, on the other hand, know the term "rising" refers to culminating dynamics within an astrological chart and not something seen in the sky. They use the movements and locations of the planets (the science of astrology) to identify the event and its physical location (the art of astrology). Furthermore, the stars that astrologers view are recorded on charts.

So which kind of rising star was it? We read on. Clearly the wise men were important enough to ride right up to King Herod's palace and gain an audience with him, which only happens with someone of great stature like another king or king's emissary. The wise men could also have been kings because that was another possible combination of professions for astrologers. In fact, in Christian tradition the magi are often referred to as kings. The wise men asked Herod where in his kingdom the King of the Jews (Messiah) has been born. The King James Version says, "Where is the child *who is born* King of the Jews," and the New Revised Standard Version says, "*has been born…*" In any event we now know two things. First we know that Jesus had already been born, and second, one may assume from Herod's response that he hadn't seen the star, nor did he know about what it indicated. In the King James Version Matthew says he was "troubled" to hear about it. The New Revised Standard Version says he was "frightened." The Greek word both interpretations are translated from is *tarasso*, which according to *Strong's* means "to agitate, trouble," clearly siding with the King James Version.

In any event none of this was good news for Herod since there is only room for one king in a kingdom. He called his chief priests and scribes. Matthew does not use the word *magos* to describe them. He asked them where the Messiah was prophesized to be born and they tell him Bethlehem. It feels safe at this point to say that no one else had seen the referenced star in the heavens. Furthermore, Matthew indicates only the wise men as those who saw the star, and the other characters do nothing to dispel that. Surely such a phenomenon, had it occurred as tradition states, would not go unnoticed, and Herod would have had his priests and scribes scour their records of prophesies and they would already be out looking for the child, not taken by surprise by the visiting astrologers.

Then something curious happened. Herod asked the wise men a specific question, wanting to know the time they first saw the star. Some translations say the "exact time" (New Standard Revised) and others say "enquired of them diligently" (King James). The Greek word that both versions translate from is *akriboo*, which *Strong's* says means "to know accurately, to do exactly." Why would Herod want to know that? There's a joke in the astrological community that if 10 "ordinary" people and one astrologer witness a car crash, all the witnesses would ask a lot of questions about what others saw. Only the astrologer would ask if anyone noted the exact time the crash happened because knowing the exact time of an event is critical for casting an accurate chart. Could it be possible that Herod and his boys wanted to do their own astrological research? It would be the practice of the times and not out of the ordinary to request such information.

We have further evidence of the role of the wise men and Herod's belief in their astrological prognostications. He had asked them to tell him where the baby was once they found him, which they didn't do, having been warned in a dream not to. Matthew reports that Herod became so enraged when he learned the wise men had departed his kingdom without telling him the baby's whereabouts and so frightened about the threat to his kingdom this baby presented that he ordered the slaughter of all boys under the age of two, additional support for the argument that Jesus had already been born.

Matthew tells us more about the star rising before the wise men, which again only they seemed to see. In fact, around the time that most biblical scholars estimate Jesus was more than likely born, there was a powerful configuration of planets. An astrologer, tracking this on paper, would see this as an indication of something special, even extraordinary. Such a configuration would go unnoticed by the non-astrologer since some of the planets involved aren't visible from earth with the naked eye, and those that are don't have a spectacular presence in the heavens. In fact, two of the main planets involved, Saturn and Jupiter, come together every 20 years and their joint appearance in the sky is decidedly unspectacular.

However people choose to interpret the story recorded in Matthew and regardless of one's religious beliefs, nearly everyone will agree that something world-changing was brought into human consciousness through the life of Jesus. The point in retelling this story is that it was a "star" that was the indicator of his birth on this planet, and it was astrologers who identified what the astrological marker meant, pointed it out to others who did not know, and then used the astrological indicators to find him.

What strikes me most about this story is that I wonder how much the world would have known of this remarkable man had the wise men not sought the manifestation of the extraordinary event about to take place, indicated by the culminating astrological indicators. Here endeth the story.

Proceeding on the path the ancient Greeks put us on, we continue to expand our knowledge of the science of the *what* of life, but we still know relatively little about the *why* of life. In spite of thousands of years of collective experience, we still don't know why the stars are indicators. Those who have studied and practiced astrology just know that they are, along with the countless numbers who seek their consultation. Similarly, physicians don't know why the body heals, they just know that it does. They have learned to use the body's symptoms as indicators to identify a course of treatment they have learned will aid in healing.

Many of astrology's detractors dismiss it because they say they are followers of science, yet they don't employ the scientific method to reach their conclusions. Those who take the time to do so—research the topic, formulate and test a hypothesis and analyze the data—often revise their original suppositions, resulting in creating some remarkable astrologers.

One of the ways we come to understand the powerful and mysterious energies operating in our universe is through stories of how they are anthropomorphized through gods and other mythical beings. I think this is the main reason the stories of the ancient gods remain with us, even though current dominant religions try to negate the power they once had in culture. Though many have tried through the centuries to kill both the gods and astrology, neither will die—perhaps because the life energies they represent are eternal.

These ancient gods have ridden with us all the way into the 21st century in their chariots and more modern vehicles. Psychologists remind us that the stories of the gods are pretty accurate pictures of the different expressions of the human psyche and that they also represent the archetypes of the collective unconscious. Classical literature, art, history, and the study of ancient myths help us better understand our origins and how they contribute to who we continue to become. This brings us to present day and how *Humanus Astrologicus* can help in that quest. So let's get started.

CHAPTER 1
HOW TO USE THIS BOOK

Humanus Astrologicus focuses on the seven "planets" in our solar system known to both ancient and modern astrologers, and what each indicates when located in the twelve signs of the zodiac. I put planets in quotation marks because even though the Sun and Moon aren't technically planets, astrology refers to them as such and puts them in a special category called "the lights" because they are the only bodies in the solar system that can light the surface of the earth and create shadows. This gives them a highlighted importance in their placements in the astrological chart.

The Signs of the Zodiac

The signs of the zodiac are always in the order presented in the following chart. The upcoming verses representing the placements of the planets in the signs will always be presented in the same order. Also included for the curious is the symbol for each astrological sign.

ASTROLOGICAL SIGN	SYMBOL
Aries the Ram	♈
Taurus the Bull	♉
Gemini the Twins	♊
Cancer the Crab	♋
Leo the Lion	♌
Virgo the Virgin	♍
Libra the Scales	♎
Scorpio the Scorpion	♏
Sagittarius the Archer	♐
Capricorn the Goat	♑
Aquarius the Water Bearer	♒
Pisces the Fish	♓

The signs of the zodiac represent different major environments of life on earth that the planets travel through and spend time in. One way to look at it is that each sign is a building that houses a particular function of life. These buildings can be a home, a school, a church, a hospital, a playground, a bank or a place of employment. More abstract environments are included, too, such as families, partnerships, lovers, friends, and necessary losses.

Each sign has its strengths and weaknesses, its standard of what constitutes accomplishment. Each has its own brand of humor, its way of making you go all gooey in love, and its concept of morality. No sign has it over any other sign although some cultures may value the traits of some signs more than others. Each sign represents a critical aspect of spirit, personality, and life in general, without which we would not be as whole or as rich. The energies of some signs are more suited to some tasks and experiences than others but that's what makes life interesting—playing the cards we're dealt.

The Planets

Every civilization had its names for planets and constellations, although Greek and Roman names are probably better known today. Astronomers in the Western world, for reasons known only to them, chose to name the planets after the Roman gods.

Following is a thumbnail chart of the gods the planets were named for, their Roman names, their corresponding Greek names, and the areas of life they rule. Please note that only the planets Sun through Saturn are included in this book. These planets are visible to the naked eye and for many centuries were the only planets used by astrologers—and quite accurately. There are branches of astrology today that still only use these seven planets because they indicate personal and interactive characteristics of the individual. The three "outer planets," Uranus, Neptune and Pluto, indicate cultural shifts in attitudes and behaviors at a generational level more than a personal level and are not included in this book.

ROMAN NAME	GREEK NAME	AREA OF RULERSHIP
Apollo	Helios	God of the Sun
Diana	Artemis	Goddess of the Moon
Mercury	Hermes	Messenger of the gods
Venus	Aphrodite	Goddess of love and beauty
Mars	Ares	God of war
Jupiter	Zeus	King of the gods
Saturn	Cronus	God of time, the Earth

Each of the planets has a distinct personality in astrology, reflecting its role in mythology. The next chart provides a thumbnail sketch of what each one represents in the astrological chart. These descriptions will be further expanded upon in the chapters on the planets. The symbol for each planet used by both astrologers and astronomers is also included.

PLANET	LIFE AREA INDICATED	SYMBOL
Sun	Who you are, your foundation	☉
Moon	How you respond emotionally	☽
Mercury	Who you say you are, how you communicate	☿
Venus	What you want and value	♀
Mars	Energy, drive, how you go after what you want	♂
Jupiter	How you expand consciousness, learn	♃
Saturn	Your limitations and how you overcome them	♄

Planets maintain their core personalities as they move through the astrological signs just as our personalities remain basically consistent wherever we go. However, how the personality is expressed is modified by the circumstances we are in. For instance, we're most relaxed and ourselves when we're at home. When we go to work our behaviors conform to a different structure required there, or they're supposed to anyway. We act differently still when on a date or visiting a strict relative's home. But we retain our individuality. Some environments are more comfortable for some personalities than others. Just as I'm a lot happier out hiking the hills than I ever was at my Aunt Emily's house, some planets have freer range to express their natural energies in some astrological signs than in others.

The placements of the planets don't cause someone to have a fiery temper, an introverted personality, a gift for healing, or a talent for writing. However, the planets are powerful indicators of those capacities. Those who know how to interpret astrological indicators can paint a pretty accurate portrait of who a person is and how he or she responds to life. *Humanus Astrologicus* gives non-astrologers a chance to paint such a portrait for themselves and the people they are interested in knowing more about—for whatever reasons.

Finding the Location of Your Planets

The fastest and easiest way to find which astrological signs your planets are in is to search on the Internet for sites that calculate astrological charts for free. There are several to choose from. When you have identified the planets' locations you may record them in the form provided at the end of this book.

Putting It All Together

Each planet has its separate chapter, starting with the Sun, with an introduction to that planet using myth to describe the tone and characteristics of that planet's basic personality and its application to life's challenges. You will note the gods were capable of amazing feats, great nobility and compassion, but they weren't always good boys and girls—far from it. They also were capable of great treachery, deceit and violence. The introduction to each chapter gives you some specifics on each god's behaviors along with helpful pointers on how those translate into your particular planetary placements, as well as how they interact with other placements.

Once you have identified the location of your planets, start with the chapter on the Sun since your Sun sign is a key signature of who you are. Read your Sun sign verse, noting which parts you think pertain to you and those that don't. There will be many points you will agree with and probably several you do not. For added input, have others close to you read your Sun sign and tell you what they think. For simplicity, the Sun sign verses also double as basic descriptors of the astrological signs. Referring to your list of your planetary locations, I suggest that if you have two or more planets in a particular sign, read the Sun Sign verse for that sign in addition to the verses describing those planets' placements. You will probably note that it identifies another theme operating in your life.

There will be some who know their ascendant or rising sign (the sign on the horizon at the time of one's birth) and want more information on it. Because ascendants have to be calculated based on the time and location of one's birth, they are not included in this book. However, for some general information you can read the Sun sign verses for the sign your ascendant is in.

After familiarizing yourself with the Sun sign verses, go on to the other chapters to read the introductions and verses on each of your planetary placements. It's helpful to have those closest to you read the verses for those placements, too, and give you feedback. As you start putting the information together, more than likely you will find vital parts of you that were missing in your Sun sign description. As you do this review here are some things to note. What planetary placements feel like they complement each other? Which ones seem to collide? Have you found an emerging theme in your life? What limitations did you discover? What strengths or talents are indicated that you may not have acknowledged before? What surprises are there?

Let's use film maker Michael Moore to exemplify how this picture comes together. People seem to either really like him or not, but most will agree that he is definitely a man on a mission. Let's see how this is exhibited by using just a few lines from each of his planetary placements including a couple of key notes from the introductory pages for each planet.

Sun in Taurus: The Sun represents who we are both at a core behavioral and mythic level as well as central themes in our lives. The pace of Taurus is methodical and deliberate. No one has been able to move Michael off his chosen path.

> *Once they have determined course*
> *They won't be moved by ox or horse.*

Moon in Pisces: The Moon indicates our emotional responses to life and represents what we feel we need at a deep emotional level. Because the Moon reflects the Sun's light it also indicates what types of emotional responses we need to see reflected back to us from others. This explains his frequent use in films of prolonged scenes of people in acute emotional distress. He needs to witness that and feels we need to witness it, too.

> *They are compassionate and buffer*
> *Those who feel deep pain and suffer;*
> *Others sympathize in theory,*
> *These folks listen 'til they're bleary.*

Mercury in Aries: Mercury represents information that is important to the person and how to communicate it. With his Mercury in Aries he especially wants to bring some form of enlightenment into the world. Mercury is also the style of communication, and in Aries he hits us hard with his message.

> *They toss ideas out to catch*
> *And land a hot debating match.*
> *They carry light where it is dark*
> *And guide us with their constant spark.*

Venus in Gemini: Venus represents what we want and what we value, because we usually only want what we value. Venus also indicates the style in which we interact in social situations. Michael's Venus in Gemini wants to connect us to each other in new ways, and he's not upset about who he offends.

> *Their social networks are extended*
> *To anyone they have befriended.*
> *They're not guided by tradition.*
> *They want to act, not seek permission.*

Mars in Capricorn: Mars, god of war, indicates how we go after what we want. He doesn't sit with his feet before the fire—he *is* the fire. Mars in Capricorn will not be denied success however success is defined. Michael's work is evidence of that.

> *Their outcomes are extraordinary.*
> *They know how to thrust and parry*
> *At any trying to control*
> *Or limit progress to their goal.*

Jupiter in Gemini: Jupiter represents where we expand ourselves and in the process seek to expand consciousness expressed in culture. With Jupiter in Gemini, Michael does this by digging up all kinds of information and making sure others know and talk about it.

> *Their deity is information;*
> *Their chariot—communication.*
> *They think ideas should be discussed,*
> *Debate and argument's a must.*

Saturn in Scorpio: The lessons of Saturn are those of facing our limitations, which are neither fun nor easy. The sign Saturn is in reveals how we learn those lessons. With Saturn in Scorpio, Michael learns his lessons first through earlier dramatic losses (revealed in his bio) and then, typical of Scorpio, rises out of his own ashes to triumphantly become what he hasn't been before.

> *Their strengths they find revealed in crisis,*
> *Peeled back like the veils of Isis.*
> *That's why they must take the trouble*
> *To sort through all their inner rubble*
> *To learn to seek change, to explore*
> *To be what they've not been before.*

And these were just a few lines from each verse. Reading each of the verses in their entirety provides a richer picture of the complex person he is, just as reviewing your verses will give you deeper insight into the complex person you are. The richness of the images in poetic form adds to this understanding.

After reading and evaluating the verses on your personal planetary placements, allow some time to digest. There isn't another vehicle in our culture at present for us to get to know ourselves quite in the same way. As an astrologer, I've learned that many people need time to chew on what's been described about them during an astrological consultation. Then a couple of weeks, maybe a few months will go by. I get a phone call saying, "You know, I've been thinking about what you said, and I really see how it fits me." The first time I had my astrological chart interpreted to me about half of it didn't sink in, but over the following months I realized how applicable the information was to me.

After you've reviewed your *Humanus Astrologicus* material ask someone close to you to read your verses and comment on what they think. Then think about what they say. We have so many unconscious patterns we may not be aware of that others clearly see.

Reading each others' verses of astrological placements is a great thing to do at a party. But beware—the situation can really get lively, especially between people who are deeply involved with each other!

Since I've rung that bell, *Humanus Astrologicus* is also helpful in better understanding the dynamics of interpersonal relationships. Anyone who has been in a committed partnership longer than two months knows there are problem areas. After 26 years of marriage my husband and I agree that we do pretty well together, but we also know that where the wheels can quickly fall off our wagon is in the style and content of our communications.

Mercury rules communication. I have Mercury in Aries and my husband has Mercury in Capricorn. I've excerpted a few lines from each verse.

My Mercury in Aries:

> *You'll quickly learn these people think*
> *Faster than the eye can blink.*
> *Their speech will tend to be quite often.*
> *There's not much they try to soften;*
> *More than that they are abrupt*
> *And frequently will interrupt.*

His Mercury in Capricorn:

> *They consider idle chatter*
> *Dumb; to them it doesn't matter.*
> *They have a very structured mind;*
> *If data coming in can't find*
> *Correct and ready storage ports*
> *They'll get pretty out of sorts.*

He will listen to me as long as he perceives that I am saying something, not just throwing words at him. Unfortunately, as the verses indicate, Mercury in Aries frequently machine-guns many words attached to thoughts that come from several different directions. Mercury in Capricorn, under this kind of siege, likes to have the file drawers of the mind open, complete with pre-labeled folders to store data for later sorting. That's how Mercury in Aries bugs Mercury in Capricorn. If you read both of these verses in their entirety you will deduce that neither placement suffers annoyances well, and therein lies another problem. Reading further in the verses reveals how Mercury in Capricorn can bug Mercury in Aries, as well as areas in which the two work well together.

Humanus Astrologicus can give you a different take on why you like the people you like, and why you don't like others. But it doesn't stop there. This type of analysis can help deepen our perceptions of people beyond what superficially appear to be quirks of personality to that of accepting them as simply exhibiting states of being. For instance, get the birth date of someone who annoys you at work, and then look up that person's planetary placements. See if you don't get a deeper understanding of him or her after "walking around in the moccasins" of learning what that person's emotional response is, what information is important to him or her, what that person really wants and values, how he or she pursues those desires, learns, and deals with limitations and challenges. Then compare them to what your planets indicate about you. More than likely you'll find your original perceptions altered. The real goal of using this information is to increase understanding and tolerance, both toward you and others. Remember, there could be people looking up *your* planets.

I could give many more examples but nothing will be as interesting as the verses that pertain to your astrological configuration and those of the people in your lives. So take advantage of this new resource, and above all—have fun!

CHAPTER 2
THE SUN

The Sun is the radiant center of our solar system, fueling and sustaining all life within it. All other planets in our solar system shine only with his reflected light. He is king of our universe and ruler of the day sky. The Sun was and continues to be associated with many cultures' religions, and throughout history the Sun has been associated with kings. Until only a few centuries ago the fates of all subjects in a kingdom were tied to the fate of their king. They could only have life by his grace. However, it is also in the Sun's light that we distinguish one form from another and perceive subtle shades of differences among each one. As history progresses so does light increasingly shine on individual identity and development.

In mythology the Sun was larger than any god, so no Greek or Roman god was large enough to be him but could only represent him. Apollo was the god most often associated with the Sun. It was his task to drive the chariot that pulled the Sun out of the sea each morning for his daily journey across the heavens, then back to his resting place for the night.

The Sun is associated with the metal gold, the most valuable metal in the ancient world. Gold has the unique property of not tarnishing. Likewise, the Sun's placement in the astrological chart represents the foundation of our being that can never be defiled, the core at the heart of each of us that belongs only to us and our creator, however that creator is defined.

The astrological sign of the Sun indicates our core personality and behavioral traits, and represents our overall consciousness. There are billions of people on this planet and only 12 signs, so clearly we share our Sun signs with millions of others. However, each life form is unique to the universe. Just as closer examination reveals that each blade of grass is different from other blades of grass and no two snowflakes are alike, each person has unique qualities. While we share many traits with others in that sign, every individual brings his or her personal stamp to their Sun sign expressions.

The Sun is classified as one of the seven "personal planets" described in this book. However, because the Sun is the center around which all other planets revolve, the sign he is in is the platform from which all other planets give their expressions. One way to think of it is that the Sun is the bulb in theater lights and the other planets are the different colored filters placed over the lights to project a specific mood on the stage, or to enhance an actor's particular expression. Sometimes the colored filters are so muted that they aren't immediately evident, and other times they are so intense that the originating light doesn't shine as brightly through them. That is why the Sun sign verses are longer than the verses for the other planetary placements. Each starts with the personal day-to-day behavioral characteristics and ends with the mythic core and purpose of that sign.

No one will identify with everything in their Sun sign verses, and some may identify a lot more than others. Some may say, "Oh, that isn't me," but might be surprised if they let those closest to them read their verses and listen to the feedback. Reading the other planetary placements will fill in a lot of holes of what isn't evident in the Sun sign.

The Sun sign verses are listed in their order in the zodiac. The dates covering each Sun sign are indicated at the beginning of each Sun sign, starting with Aries which begins the zodiac on March 21, the spring equinox.

The fastest and easiest way to find which astrological sign your Sun is in is to search on the Internet for sites that calculate astrological charts for free. My Sun is in the sign of _____.

SUN IN ARIES (THE RAM)
March 21–April 19

They love to lead us from the dark,
Inspiring us with constant spark
To boldly go out and explore
Where no one's ever gone before,
Making us feel small and feckless
While they're being bold and reckless.

They feel that they've great things to do
But what they are they've not a clue.
They only know they must go on
Through darkest night into new dawn.

They like to be the people who
Get somewhere first, but number few
In long term management employment.
It doesn't give them much enjoyment,
But if some duty calls they'll stay
Although you've got to let them play.

They talk a lot, plus they're up front,
So you've been warned—they're pretty blunt.
Snappy with a fast comeback,
Long attention spans they lack.
They're not afraid to be caught snoring
If the goings-on are boring.

Rarely do they think or pause
Before defending each lost cause.
A few may seem the timid lamb
But they become the mighty ram
Using great ferocity
When fighting some atrocity.

They never seem to quite mature
Yet still they have a strange allure.
They can enrage us, then disarm
Us with their most peculiar charm.

They're drawn to anything that's new
And may not stay too long with you.
They're not inclined to mope or grieve,
They just pack up their things and leave.

They tell the truth quite easily
And seldom will act weasely.
With Aries one should not forget
That what you see is what you get.

They're trusting, often quite naïve
And can be easy to deceive.
As infants of the zodiac
They do not always stay on track.
They're thought by some as narcissistic.
When they get mad they go ballistic.

Most Aries are so quizzical
About the metaphysical
And think that it is truly tragic
When folks don't believe in magic.

They only need a gentle nudge
To drop what could become a grudge
Except when there has been betrayal;
Anger then goes off the scale
And either ends in fire or ice.
If it's ice you'll pay a price
For Aries' ice is permanent
As stars are in the firmament.

Keeping contact with a phone
They walk through much of life alone.
Don't feel sorry for them, though,
They're far too self-absorbed to know.

As Prometheus stole fire
From the gods and caught their ire
All so he could light man's path,
Bold Aries' spirit raises wrath
In those who have control or clout.

Now try to figure this one out—
So fantastic as it seems
They weave us tapestries of dreams
With trailing mists from Pisces' seas
They spin from life's deep mysteries
That they bring forward to each day
As light to help us find our way.
This comes through them from way down deep.
It's given to them in their sleep.

It's such a contrast, though, to all
That up-front wit and grit and gall.
Don't burn yourself, for each one carries
Fire—that's the soul of Aries.

SUN IN TAURUS (THE BULL)
April 20–May 20

Once they have determined course
They won't be moved by ox or horse,
Or any means used to distract
Like reason, argument or fact.

Others may in panic scurry,
Taurus will so slowly hurry.
They must weigh these things a bit.
It's not that they're not quick of wit,
For in some crisis if there's need
They can act with lightning speed,
But they must know their sweat and toil
Plant seeds that grow in fertile soil.
That's why they plod along the trail
Of each small, single last detail.

They're steady and they're pretty humble.
They pick themselves up if they fumble.
They won't drop out of the race,
Not even if they're in last place.

Don't miscalculate their calm;
This part of them's a ticking bomb.
Their mellow eyes and placid gazes
May belie their moody phases.
Mostly they're serene and mellow
But now and then they'll really bellow,
And if they do, if you've much sense
You'll run and jump the nearest fence
And don't come back until you're clear
It's safe to once again come near.

They like to rest a well trimmed hoof
In comfort 'neath a stately roof.
They aren't the first to moralize
Nor lead the herd on exercise.
They take the time to loll and laze;
You'll need a hand grenade to raise
Them off those pillows, beds or couches.
Then they can be awful grouches.

They're very good at social graces
But prefer the kinds of places
Where they have their loved ones near,
Can kick off shoes and have a beer.

In spite of all of their resistance,
They daily celebrate existence.
One of many ways they measure
Happiness is by each pleasure.
They love all beauty and the arts
Which touch them deeply in their hearts.
They like best things that they can touch,
They like them very, very much.

It acts for them as healing salve
To inventory what they have.
Their love of comfort is amazing.
Yes, they're rather fond of grazing;
Many of them run toward stout,
But do not rule the thin ones out
For whether they are thin or fat

These people know where good food's at.
If they like a dish a lot
Then they'll cook a real big pot
And eat from it all through the week
Making those they live with shriek.

If they've abandoned earthly things
To chant, wear robes and crystal rings,
Know that they are never shirking
Duty, loved ones, even working.
They'll just do this crazy stuff
(Which in their youth they labeled "fluff")
When money's made, been banked and stored,
They're in retirement or bored.

There's not a thing they can't endure
If it makes loved ones more secure,
And even though they're strong and stoic
They don't need to be heroic.
Rarely will they take the praise
For the crops they help to raise.

They nurture fire deep in the mud
That touches hearts and warms the blood.
Their careful work will send down roots
That sprout and grow new tender shoots.
Ploddingly they till earth for us,
For that's the way of steady Taurus.

SUN IN GEMINI (THE TWINS)
May 21–June 21

They will have the most respect
For those with higher intellect.
They're clever and they are superb
At smartly placing noun with verb.
Their hands are quicker than our eyes,
Their mouths are faster with replies.

They have a host of inner voices
To assist them in their choices.
Please remember, they are twins;
One will scowl, the other grins,
Or in some meeting one will scan
To give the other time to plan.
If you're confused each time you meet
They have a different way they greet,
Remember two come in a pair;
Just figure out which twin is there.

When you see them with their peers
They look younger than their years.
They're flexible, a great pinch hitter
And they really love to twitter.
They're excited by new games
And they know all their neighbors' names.

Tradition's not their guiding star,
Not if it shackles who they are.
They're casual about the rules
If they think they're made by fools.
They don't wait to get consent;
They triumph through experiment.

People think they are confused;
They're not at all, they're just diffused.
They can make a choice and pick
Solutions with a speed so quick,
So often when they gather speed
The rest of us may feel the need
To pause a minute and pull back
To see which train is on which track.
To Gemini that's such a bore,
They always keep track of the score.

It's pretty hard to tick them off,
They shrug their shoulders and click off.
But do not think this can't be done
Or you will be the sorry one,
For if you make them mad you've sprung

A trap releasing acid tongue.
Then with precision surgical
And flow almost liturgical
They'll tangle you in verbal wire
With barbs that just increase your mire.

Their relationships unravel
If one partner doesn't travel;
But to travel, on one hand,
Just may invite a one night stand,
But then it's always so exciting
To have frequent reuniting
With one's partner or one's spouse
In one's own beloved house.
They need freedom or they die,
This two-for-one sign, Gemini.

It doesn't matter what their race
There is a lightness to the face,
Distinctive qualities of skin
That seem to let more light come in.
But shadows quickly can replace
The light that plays upon the face.

A part of them must always be
In flight with winged Mercury
Who is magician to the gods
And thus increases well the odds
That his prized magical caduceus
Of the mind can then seduce us
Into thinking that what is is not
And what is not is best forgot.
You missed that, did you, flew right by?
You must keep up with Gemini.

They teach us that we must explore
All the passageways, each door
Through which, with great impunity,
We start our search for unity.
Their findings they are glad to share
But of this fact please be beware—

You must catch them on the fly
To talk at all with Gemini.

SUN IN CANCER (THE CRAB)
June 22–July 21

They love a thing so old it creaks,
So they tend to like antiques.
Somewhere back there in the past
Are keys to things that really last,
So they've memories like elephants.
They'll take comfort over elegance,
And one could write up reams and tomes
About how much they love their homes.

To them a laugh acts like a cure,
You'll hear it frequently, I'm sure,
An antidote to cycling moods
Along with some appealing foods;
That's why you'll often find them munching.
Shoulders slightly forward hunching,
Long and swinging arms and hands,
They look like sideling crabs in sand.

They tend to hide, feel insecure
When conditions are unsure.
Instead of saying, "Go to hell,"
They may pull into a shell
Where they're inclined to brood and sulk,
Eat lots of food and increase bulk.
They move sideways, rarely toward.
They have a tendency to hoard
And like no other signs they stash
And save for rainy days some cash.

In all decisions they will link
What they feel with what they think,
Relying just as much on smarts
As on the contents of their hearts.

At home and work they care for us.
They keep us safe, they make a fuss.
They're gifted how they manage staff.
They're good with numbers, charts and graphs.
When someone with a Cancer Sun
Tells you that, "This can't be done
Until this such-and-such is changed
Or thingity-bob is rearranged,"
If you ignore this you're in trouble
And this is how you make it double.
They told you once, they told you twice
And when they spoke they were so nice
In their own way that's indirect
(And for this you will learn respect)
About this job they worked so hard,
They ground it out by inch and yard
Before they passed it on to you
So you could do your part there, too.
If you had listened then instead
You'd not be wishing you were dead.

If you harm a Cancer's child
Their responses can be wild.
It's not just children they adore
But vegetable or rock or spore
If they gave birth to them somehow.
Is this picture clearer now?

To love a Cancer you will be
Entwined with all their family,
And you'll need patience much like Job,
They may be scattered 'round the globe.
If from their family they're estranged
You'll wish conditions could be changed
Since it's like living with a ghost.
For Cancer, family matters most.

They're at home in deepest night
And understand things out of sight.
They teach us that our darkest time
Just shows where we must start to climb

And that the dark is not to fear;
It only means conception's near.

They're like rivers, they're like oceans
In their constant rhythmic motions
With the swirling of the tide
Touching feelings deep inside.
Both men and women are in tune
With each new cycle of the moon.
It depends upon the hour
For their magnitude of power
From slow creeping snails of night
To leaping whales almost in flight.
Don't think you can predict this though,
It changes as tides come and go.
You'll learn their rhythms are the answer
When you spend lots of time with Cancer.

SUN IN LEO (THE LION)
July 22–August 21

So like the Sun god high above,
Apollo, sending light and love,
They're emanating solar rays
With each grand gesture, stellar phrase.
It can be very hard to swallow,
Leos acting like Apollo,
How their egos send us reeling
Yet they somehow stay appealing.
Each ignores his own life's mess
Yet runs our lives with great finesse.

Don't pat a Leo on the head
Or you will wish that you were dead.
They're very conscious of their hair
Even when no longer there.
If their purr-fect manes aren't right
They'll hide to keep them out of sight

Until they're fixed again quite grand—
It's best that others understand.

Each Leo is a lion pride,
All elements each has inside:
The cute and playful little cub
Who rolls and wants a tummy rub,
The mama who's out stalking kill,
The papa snoring on his hill.
So cubs that play with you right now
Can turn and stalk you down for chow.
It doesn't have to happen though,
Just let the Leo steal the show.

As robes and crowns adorn the king,
Leos drape themselves in bling.
Regardless of the Leo's age
They love to be in center stage.
What more could any person ask
Than be in Leo's light to bask,
To wait on them and pledge allegiance
To these awesome feline regents?
Still, often loved ones may complain
That they don't share in Leo's reign
And have been granted lesser rights
As roving moons and satellites
Around their lion's solar flare.
With Leo nothing can compare.

At times we find a timid cat
Who hasn't found where its roar's at.
It seems to you as if they hide
But if you dare attack their pride
You'll find a cat out on the prowl
To track you down with deadly growl.

That which really fuels their fires
Is following their hearts' desires,
And with their energy abounding
What they accomplish is astounding.
But at times their goals get hazy

As they really can be lazy;
You're just as apt to find them snoring
As you are to hear them roaring.

If you want their power and passion
To evolve in gentler fashion,
Work with lion cubs on taming,
Not on punishment and shaming.
When they pull a stunt inane,
Point out appearances; they're vain.

Of who they are they've not much sense
Unless they have an audience.
Like children learning something new
They have to play it back to you,
Confident of what they've learned
But not yet sure of what that earned.

They can't contribute, do their parts
Until awakening their hearts.
Until that time they need to seek
The spotlight, show how they're unique.
When their egos take a blow
Its purpose is so they can know
Unconscious patterns to work through,
Their inner lions to subdue.
They only do their very best
Once they complete this inner quest.

They must track the path of soul
Back to where its source is whole.
The Sun god brought to us our spirit,
And when with Leo we are near it.

SUN IN VIRGO (THE VIRGIN)
August 22–September 22

They always will precisely show
You how to do it, nicely, though.
Each displays an innate poise

Which starts as little girls and boys,
And noted for sobriety
They keep intact propriety.

Be careful that you don't conclude
That a Virgo is a prude.
They'll throw convention to the winds
For theirs, not someone else's sins.
They have a very earthy passion
Which they show you in their fashion.
Don't be fooled 'cause they're genteel,
These folks are born with spines of steel.

They worry more about their health
Than the status of their wealth.
They are obsessed with food and diet
(Bake it, please, don't ever fry it)
Counseling if you had jogged
Your arteries would not be clogged,
Or if you'd try this herbal tea
You wouldn't have that painful knee.

It's true their bodies run toward lean
And yes, they like things sparkling clean.
For sure, you'll often hear them mutter
How they truly can't stand clutter.
Don't be fooled by this facade;
They have a trait that some find odd.
When Virgo's ordered coin is flipped
You'll see that chaos there has ripped.
Refrigerator food's so old
They learn to catalogue the mold.
It seems somehow incredible
There's stuff in there that's edible.

When some plan has run amok
And they are for the moment stuck,
They'll wade through papers, books and more
With which they litter up the floor.
They don't escape to Pisces' mists,
Instead they write up reams of lists

To cite exacting estimations
Scheduling order restorations.

When relationships go wrong
Many tend to stay too long,
Thinking they can make it right
When what they should do is take flight.

They will get into a bind
If they don't balance body/mind.
When there's something new to learn
It makes their insides hurt and churn.

They don't seek the bright spot light;
They just want to get things right.
If things don't work they want to change them.
They'd be glad to rearrange them
And can, incidentally,
Show you how to incrementally.
If a project is well analyzed,
The budget's not been compromised,
One may assume that, ergo,
It is managed by a Virgo.

They know that in creative arts
The whole is greater than its parts,
And if those parts aren't neatly placed
The whole will surely be defaced.

They've magic powers in their hands
To fix machines or harvest lands,
To treat the sick, do other arts
That heal our minds and heal our hearts.
While other signs may show more verve
These Virgos have a need to serve,
Preparing us in great detail
How to relate on broader scale.

They love all the furry creatures
As companions and good teachers.
Virgos love the things of earth,

Promote and understand their worth.
They seem to have a magic wand
That touches rock and tree and pond.
They show the order nature teaches
Puts perfection in our reaches.
A call to service they won't shirk;
Virgos show us how to work.

SUN IN LIBRA (THE SCALES)
September 23–October 22

They want us all to be aware
That life should have good grace, be fair.
With benign and pleasant faces
They excel in social graces,
Conscious of impressions made
Even if their nerves are frayed.

They love to see themselves extended
To new people they've befriended
Which gives them chances for comparing
All the different ways of sharing.
They can follow many themes
And have great patience with extremes.

They think they're such a peaceful dove.
It's not the battles that they love,
But they can argue with great flair;
Jump in the middle if you dare.
When they ramp up to orate
They're without equal in debate.
They won't scowl or even frown,
They simply talk and wear you down,
Recalling words, how they were spoken,
In a chain that is unbroken
Back to when the world was new.
As they then play it back to you
You'll feel you're sinking in a marsh;
The scales of Libra can be harsh.

Oh, I could really tell some tales
Of Libras balancing their scales,
Like if they say, "Let's see a show,"
Don't grab your coat and start to go
Because they must evaluate
Many times and then restate
The reasons they would like to go
But also why they shouldn't, though.

Some may say derisively
They act so indecisively,
But this you really shouldn't do
Because it simply isn't true.
Like judges who before they act
Must consider every fact,
All the issues Libras see
Dance in their minds concurrently.
Until they're sorted for decision
They will feel a great division.
Though your patience is in shreds
And all that's left are tattered threads,
The Libras feel so good that they
Reviewed all options in the fray.

Much preferring things abstract
They deal in theory more than fact.
They're not emotive, they are mental
And at times can be judgmental.
One can't really call it flaw,
Their strict adherence to the law,
For where the Libras get their force
Is law that's from the highest source.

If you've just seen their pleasant sides
You've only taken half their rides.
Mostly if fair Libra wails
It's all because they've tipped their scales.
It's not their fault their scales are tilted;
Well, you see, they just got jilted
Or room colors were not right
Or lighting was too dim (or bright).

Unbalanced settings make them ill,
They must go home and take a pill.

Although we all are disappointed
When those with our love anointed
Soon reveal a human being,
Not the gods we first were seeing,
Libra feels a deeper wound.
They thought they were so well in-tuned
And share with us their self-berating.
Karmically they rule relating.

They act for us as constant voice
To speak the consequence of choice.
Their gift to us is the ensurance
That we will maintain endurance
To ease the pain of life alone
By seeking kinship on our own.
As friend or lover, sister, brother,
Libra brings us to each other.

SUN IN SCORPIO (THE SCORPION)
October 23–November 21

Life's a chessboard, they're the master.
They can strategize much faster
Than anyone can ever know.
They're careful not to let it show.

They have these voices warm and tender
Which can change and quickly render
You a helpless quaking gel,
And they don't even have to yell.

They're quick to feel but slow to show,
Their ticking bombs will one day blow.
Nature made them quite intense
So to disguise this built a fence.
We know it as a poker face
That stares quite blankly out in space.

29

Some have this propensity
To hide their eyes' intensity
Behind a stylish pair of glasses
Just so they won't scare the masses.

At times forgetting that they're mortal,
They're always searching for a portal
Through which lies the heart of things,
The prize they hope each journey brings.
So they're as apt to set their sights
Upon the depths as well as heights,
Penetrating all life's strata
Probing for some hidden data.

Parties? They don't quite enjoy them
Because so many folks annoy them.
They've different ways they socialize,
Probing deeply in your eyes
Or more pointedly with speech
To see what depths in you they'll reach,
Or better yet make you reveal
Some things you've tried hard to conceal.

Talking with them can be dicey.
They are either warm or icy.
Their attitudes can be quite stony
If they think that you're a phony
Or if they just plain don't like you.
Take heart—it's rare that they will strike you.

They're loyal once you've passed their test,
But what that was they won't divest.
Of private things they rarely speak
But you might get a little peek.
It's with their eyes they let you know
Through which their feelings overflow.

They're known to most as super sleuth
Because they sort out lies from truth.
And if you are mysterious
It makes them, oh, so curious,

But never overplay your hand,
For if they ever think you've planned
To drive them nuts, my friends, you must
Be told that you then lose their trust,
And that is not the way to go
Believe me, folks, with Scorpio.

They go where their deep passion takes them
Even if the journey breaks them.
If they find that they're in hell
They fight their way out and don't tell
Who else they found there suffering;
They'll give those souls some buffering.
It's easy for them to remain
At length with those who are in pain
Because they've had more than their share
Of troubles that are hard to bear.
They know like no one else of pain
But also like no others gain.
They move through pain at glacial speed;
It's hard to watch them slowly bleed,
But then they rise from mortal clashes
Like the Phoenix from its ashes.

They need to feel they have control
No matter what their life or role.
While others seek release from stress,
A Scorpio goes full-court press.
The mission charged to Scorpio
Is dive real deep and go below
To drown in murky pools of death,
Then find new seeds for life and breath—
No breezy conversation piece.
It's hard for them to find release.

Some of them may go to church
But all find truth through deep research.
When it comes their time to die
Their last word uttered will be, "Why?"
Regretting all that they don't know,
Because, you see, it's Scorpio.

SUN IN SAGITTARIUS *(THE ARCHER)*
November 22–December 21

When they speak they blurt out gaffs
That give us all such belly laughs.
They're shamelessly bereft of tact
When telling us some point in fact
Which they so often will espouse
With both feet firmly in their mouths.

You'll know when one is in the crowd,
Their voices carry, can be loud.
They often cut a lot of slack
And do not mind if you talk back.
They lead us off on long digressions
With exuberant expressions
Which each piercingly delivers
With some arrows from their quivers.

They often run a little late
But not because they ruminate,
It's just this meeting was protracted
And, you see, they got distracted.

Remember, please, they're partly satyrs,
Seeing love as banquet platters
From which they will freely pick
A fling or two that's fun and quick.
You'll need a leash that's long and strong
To keep the Archer close for long
Unless you get them when they're older,
Then they'll stay close by your shoulder.

Much more active than intense
They scorn the concept known as "fence."
They're prone to lots of wandering
And also to some squandering.
They, with boastful pride, confess
To their latest hot excess.

They're as adept at breaking horses
As at complex physics courses.
They will shift from clown to sage
Even way past middle age.
Surprisingly they can be calm,
Diffusing perfectly some bomb
With wit and charm and poise and grace
And utter gravity of face;
But once the crisis passes peak
They're then inclined to tweak your cheek,
Get up and gallop down the hall
Too fast and smash into some wall.

They can be gentle as the sparrows
But they also have sharp arrows.
Don't take to heart all that they say.
They're generous in every way,
So even when they do flare up
They'll still share their plate and cup.
Remind them of their giving hearts,
Their arrows turn to rubber darts.

Truth is what they want to find
Through unrestricted use of mind.
Their zeal for life can overwhelm.
Remind them when they're at the helm
The way to focus their decisions
Is putting into plans their visions.
You'll have fun along the way,
These people die if they can't play.
They're utterly gregarious,
Those born in Sagittarius.

Propelled on pointed centaur hooves
They seldom follow traveled grooves.
Instead they track the arrow's flight
Through wild and unexplored dark night
Where they enjoy a mythic revel
At the god and goddess level
Joining Jupiter and Isis,
Venus, Vulcan, Dionysus,

Bringing appetite that's hearty
To this higher world party
Where they argue with the deities
And wrestle angels with such ease.

That's why they don't run out of fire
That fuels them so they can inspire
Us to channel truth as source
To help us choose our own best course
From choices which were, by and by,
First introduced by Gemini.
The search will sure be various,
But fun with Sagittarius.

SUN IN CAPRICORN (THE GOAT)
December 22–January 20

They always have the perfect plan
To help each woman, child, and man.
They will tightly run the show
And like a dam control the flow.
Mastering those things they choose,
It's in their plans to never lose.

They have these raging inner fires
Fueled by drives and strong desires,
But rocky crusts prevent the flow
Of lava that just wants to blow.
So if you catch them in repose
They look like stone from head to toes.

It's not their best loved kind of fun
To work in teams to get things done;
Oh, they can do it if there's need
But they prefer to take the lead.

They like to live a cut above
And take good care of those they love.

For many of them it seems normal
To entertain in ways quite formal.

You'll have to prove to them your merit
By your actions while they ferret
Out those reams of evidentials
To support your life's credentials.

Most won't squander funds on poker,
They'll invest them with a broker.
They don't tend to be the type
That's suckered in by lots of hype.
The gifts they give to those they cherish
Won't be flashy, won't be garish.
Other signs and their flamboyance
Lead to Capricorn's annoyance
Since no one really needs panache,
They think, for making lots of cash.
Weighted down with sense of duty
They can bring home lots of booty.

They can act removed and huffy
And at times they're downright stuffy.
You'll know when you have ticked them off,
They do not move or speak or cough
But glare at you 'neath beetle brow
And make you wish you could somehow
Just find yourself a safety zone
Instead of under their big stone.

If you're linked with Capricorn
Then of this point I have to warn:
Be sure to never ridicule
Or try to make them look the fool.
This lesson you will have to learn
Or else they'll give you quite a burn.

They seem more solemn than their peers
Especially in early years,
But as they age one often finds
They act as if they've lost their minds,

For once you've tapped their humor vein
You'll wonder if they're really sane.
To see their crack-up zany wit
You have to know them for a bit
Before they let it out. You know,
It's hard for them to let things go.

They don't ignore the things sublime,
They're just so conscious of the time.
They're always seeking liberation
From their own administration.
They must learn that they don't own
Those structures they build out of stone
And come to see that they're just skin
Around the temple built within.

They bring to form the various
Bright dreams of Sagittarius.
When we've tracked some falling star
They show us how things really are.
When we're all wrecked on rocks and shoals
They redirect us to our goals.
With patience that can make one weep
They teach us how we have to keep
A balance of life's driving force
With how to choose our proper course.
If you need guidance when you're torn
It's best to seek a Capricorn.

SUN IN AQUARIUS (THE WATER BEARER)
January 21–February 19

You think they're there when they are not.
They'll often tell you, "I forgot."
Their minds go to some future place
Where they are able to embrace
New ideas just taking form
Which they will use to change some norm.

Though they're the ones who rearrange
Conditions so we can have change,
They act like bees defending hives
If you attempt to change their lives.
They're stubborn as the devil.
They want playing fields all level
And they want no one left behind.
To those in pain they're very kind.

They'll unravel the enigma
Of what constitutes a stigma
And they'll go to any ends
To help their weird and varied friends,
All these philanthropic elves
Who live so near the edge themselves.

They happily pontificate
And lecture more than they debate.
Around the planet they will lope
To bring to light some global hope,
Yet loved ones get them in a snit
Attempting to make them commit
To household tasks they can't abide,
Like when they'll take the trash outside.

For all their rallying to cause
They have some teeny little flaws,
Like their tempers can be frightening
When they hit like bolts of lightning.
They lack tolerance for stupid
And drag their heels in meeting Cupid.

In romance they're far from meek
Though love with them's like hide-and-seek
Because you are in competition
With each new cause and coalition,
New technologies released—
What happened to that great love feast?

Their minds work so electrically,
They live their lives eclectically.

Their eyes beam this electric hue
That seems to penetrate through you.
Their wild hair will tend to wave,
They spend far better than they save.

They either cook with great finesse
Or else they make a shocking mess;
They make concoctions so God-awful
One may wonder if they're lawful.
All who love them have yelled, "Halt,"
When they start reaching for the salt.

They prey just like a vulture
On outmoded parts of culture
To tear down structures that were born
And formed in stone by Capricorn.
In this rubble they'll recover
Newness which they there discover.

They look forward, rarely back.
They do not run much with the pack.
Determined not to ever fail,
They're lonely knights who seek the Grail.
They hope a good companion rides
Staying closely at their sides,
But if their friends cannot keep up
They still pursue that sacred cup.

Like angels or the avatars
Who visit from beyond the stars,
They bring their visions to our land
Which largely we misunderstand.

Their hearts aren't where they energize,
That's hidden more behind their eyes.
If you share their electric world
Some thrilling joys will be unfurled.
The future's where they'll carry us,
This highly charged Aquarius.

SUN IN PISCES (THE FISH)
February 20–March 20

They're most happy when in service.
If forced to race they can get nervous
Not because they won't compete,
But when the others crank up heat
They must find value in that race
Or they may sit and stare in space.

Their daily rhythms change with mood
From social whirl to solitude.
They need a lot of time alone
When they can read, space out, atone.
They're chatty with most everyone
But they won't really look for fun,
So partners or the ones they marry
Will act as social secretary.

Though they've a gift for witticism.
They have thin skin for criticism,
So make sure that you don't take pokes
That target them the butt of jokes.

When they have to choose a side
They'll use feelings to decide.
For all the ways that they are dreamers
You'll find they equally are schemers
With subtle ways that they resist
And equally how they persist.

When they bear loved ones' abuses
They tend to offer up excuses.
Though you've known your Fish for years,
They've soothed away your pains and tears,
In this they're much like Scorpio—
There's much about them you won't know.

They often dwell on past regrets;
The Fish forgives but not forgets.

If you're going to do them wrong
Their recall for those slights is long;
They carry both the bad and good
All the way from childhood.

With all nature they commune
As notes join sweetly in a tune.
They love the sea, the lakes and pools
And value them as much as jewels.
Even when they're old and totter
These fish love to be in water.

There's loneliness they must endure,
Designed to purge them, make them sure
That nothing ever can dilute
Ideals they hold as absolute.

Often when you're with the Fish
They make you feel they have a wish
That they could travel, oh, so far
Out to some strange and distant star,
Or else you feel they'd like to be
In hidden caves beneath the sea
To comb a wild seahorse mane
Where Merman and his daughters reign.

It is so much more likely, though,
That you will see them in some show
Where they are free to do their parts
Through talents in creative arts.
They seem to have with great profusion
Talent to create illusion.

They know the downward side of life,
About the wars and greed and strife
And always seem to understand,
Are glad to lend a helping hand.

Here is one of their conclusions:
Separations? Just illusions.
Everybody is connected

In ways not seen but still affected.
They're born to be the people who
Will part the veils so we see through
Both worlds, the unseen and the seen
Which they feel they're caught between.
How to bridge them is their choice,
A process hard for them to voice.

Pisces learn their mystic notions
Swimming in the cosmic oceans,
But living in those mighty currents
Can serve to act as strong deterrents
To playing in life's scrimmages
With their ideals and images.
The wisdom used for mystic crises
Is carried deep in souls of Pisces.

CHAPTER 3
THE MOON

The Moon is sister to the Sun and queen of the night sky. Together they constitute the two "lights" in the heavens. Even though the Moon and planets shine with the Sun's reflected radiance, planets are not considered lights because their illuminations are not sufficient to light the surface of the earth.

As with the Sun, the Moon was larger than any one god. She is represented in mythology by the goddess Diana. The sibling relationship of shared power over the earth by the Sun and Moon is symbolized by the relationship of Diana to Apollo, the Sun god. They are sister and brother, twins in fact. A symbol in nature of their relationship is that while we know the Sun is much larger than the Moon, from earth they appear to be the same size in the sky.

Diana is also known as the goddess of the hunt and is often depicted with her bow and arrow chasing wild game. The hunter can also become the hunted. The Sun and Moon daily play that out as the rising Moon appears to chase the Sun from the sky and several hours later, he then chases her from the heavens.

Albert Camus observed that there are two worlds, the world of day and the world of night, posing, "Which is the real world?" During the light of day we feel secure in our surroundings, but at night, especially when moonlight unifies everything with its wash of white and silver, nothing has its daytime familiarity. Howling is done at the Moon, not the Sun. Ghost stories are only scary at night around the campfire, but seem silly during the day. It is at night that our emotions are exaggerated. It is at night that our fears come out. It is at night that we feel more pulled to the mystical, to the magical. And it is at night that we dream, sowing the seeds for what we hope to bring to light during the day.

In astrology the Sun represents our conscious behaviors and actions, while the Moon indicates our subconscious responses. This is reflected in nature by the fact that the Sun, king of the day sky, is never visible in the realm of the Moon, queen of the night sky, but she is regularly seen in his. Several days out of every month she is clearly visible in the day sky, symbolizing that our subconscious content can and does intrude upon our conscious lives in ways we may not be aware of and that can spring out in surprising ways when triggered. Only during the full Moon do the two briefly face each other and shine with equal light from opposite horizons at a time that is neither day nor night.

It is the nature of the Moon to be changeable. She is the only heavenly body to regularly show us her different faces, from brilliant full moon glory to total darkness and all phases in between. She rules the ebb and flow of earth's tides and indicates the many cycles of change and growth, from fertility to barrenness. Few aspects of ourselves are more changeable than how we may feel about something at any given moment. The sign the Moon is in is the chief indicator of our feeling nature and emotional responses. Just as the Moon reflects the Sun's light, so do our emotional responses reflect what we need to see and feel coming back to us from our environments.

The sign the moon is in also indicates the types of contacts we need to feel secure and safe, how we extend ourselves emotionally to others or protect ourselves from them. Some astrological signs are comfortable with deeply expressed feelings and need to receive the same from others. Other signs need emotional distance, preferring to objectify what they and others feel. Still others find emotions messy and uncomfortable. It should never be interpreted that people with their Moons in signs that don't express emotions freely do not feel. Everyone feels and even though it isn't always apparent they feel deeply.

The Moon is associated with mothers and families of origins. Since our ancestors preceded us on this planet, the Moon is also associated with our relationship to the past, including memory.

The Moon is the most rapidly moving planet in astrology. It only spends two and a half days in one astrological sign, making the complete round of the zodiac in less than 30 days.

The fastest and easiest way to find which astrological sign your Moon is in is to search on the Internet for sites that calculate astrological charts for free. My Moon is in the sign of _____.

MOON IN ARIES

These people don't cajole or plead,
They go after what they need.
While other signs may sulk or pout
An Aries Moon just gets it out.

Know that though they can get snappy
It doesn't mean that they're not happy,
But they need partners who are strong
If they're going to get along,

Like bullets shot out from a gun
Their energy must have its run.
They rush to meet life, they're not shy.
There's not too much that they won't try,
But routine work they do not like.
They're then inclined to take a hike.
They seem compulsive, but they're not.
They're driven, so they push a lot.
They chase desires with such speed
That they confuse a want with need.

Their childhoods were sometimes hard
Which can result in being marred
By living in a battlefield
Which in adulthood can be healed.

Like a magnet they attract
All kinds of people who will act
As angels helping them attain
Their goals, no matter how arcane.

They have to do things that are new
Which may not be involving you.
They need to track the lonely star
That keeps them moving, leads them far,
Sometimes by choice, sometimes by fate.
Know this well if you're their mate.

MOON IN TAURUS

They're emotionally stable
And are constructed to be able
To endure, it seems, most anything,
Those challenges that life can bring,
So they're least likely to have tried
To end their lives by suicide.

Their habits will be pretty fixed,
So plans for change are quickly nixed.
If you push them hard, insist,
They dig their heels in and resist.

They don't easily confide
Those troubles swirling deep inside.
They have to ruminate and stew
Before they'll trot them out to you.

Their homes are lovely and quite tasteful.
They're hoarders and they find it wasteful
To throw out what they have amassed;
To most things they will hold on fast.
Their best form of security
Is feeling with great surety
That they will have enough resources
To withstand all harmful forces.

They need pleasure which they savor,
Liking every kind of flavor,
All the textures, how they feel,
And they look forward to each meal.

That which is their deepest need
Is that they must plant a seed,
Then tend it, nurture, help it grow.
They're patient, understand that's slow.
They care more that they've tended, fed it
Than they care that they get credit.

They're steady and they persevere.
They need to have their loved ones near.
Though they're not real pliable
They surely are reliable.
They're loyal both as friend and mate
Through all the vagaries of fate.

MOON IN GEMINI

Because they keep themselves in motion
They don't get tied up in emotion.
Feelings mostly stay inside them
Not because they try to hide them,
It's just they have to percolate
Through heart to mind, then they relate
In some objectifying way
Exactly what they're going to say.

They need to talk of their reflections.
It helps them make those new connections.
You will find that they are good
At networking the neighborhood,
The gym, their schools, the coffee shop—
And they will do this all non-stop.

They're anthropologists of sorts,
Giving us the full reports
Of their many observations
Of their human explorations,
Regaling us with all their stories
Of our failures, of our glories.

When it comes to meeting change
These people have an awesome range.
When other signs get mad or pout
These folks say, "Let's talk this out."
Then they will objectify
That which they seek to rectify.
Still, you can tell when they're upset;
They bark out something they regret.

When someone's in a moody phase
They tend to go their separate ways,
But when someone's deep in pain
They'll sit with them and will remain
Until the crisis has moved on.
Then like the wind, they, too are gone.

Although there's much that they will tell,
Few will know them very well.
And as they age they learn to find
And claim their hearts long trapped in mind.

MOON IN CANCER

If you need them, they are there;
It doesn't matter when or where.
Face it now, they are our mothers,
Whether they are sisters, brothers.
Some will like this mother love
But some may call it smother love.

In sharing feelings they're not shy,
But like the Moon up in the sky
Their feeling states will wax and wane.
That's who they are, they don't explain.
They need to be alone a lot
At home, and on the phone a lot.
And then they'll take you by surprise
And make huge plans to socialize.

They love to mix and play with foods
To match their often changing moods.
They have a tendency toward drama
When they sustain some hurt or trauma.
Many tend to hold on fast
To things that happened in the past.

They feel secure and most respected
When with others they're connected.
Although they need friends they retreat,
So you should call and say, "Let's meet,"
For if they're left alone too long
They think their friendship isn't strong.
Then they are so delighted
To discover they're invited,
So please be sure that you have heeded
That they require to be needed.
This be sure to emphasize
As you gaze deeply in their eyes.

MOON IN LEO

While outwardly they may be shy,
Be aware that may belie
Their inner need that they engage
Once they're put on center stage.
Even when they're just informing,
They can't help it—they're performing.
If perchance someone ignores them,
They feel hurt, it simply floors them.
They're not happy cast as flunkies.
On top of that they're action junkies.

They will choose some high ideal
And cling to it with fiery zeal,
And though it may seem quite outrageous
Their energy will be contagious.
They need to be those who inspire
And light other people's fire.

They're very difficult to sway,
Are clever how they get their way.
They are so sincerely charming
And their air is quite disarming.

They must separate their feelings
From their egos in their dealings
For their warmth and generosity
Can come mixed with some pomposity.

They must keep dignity intact
With every gesture, phrase and act.
Life to them is super size.
It's hard for them to compromise.
That's why they get aloof and haughty
When they're caught at being naughty.
Don't attack them in their pride.
It hurts them and they hide inside.

Life with them's both bold and sweet—
Just be sure you don't compete.

MOON IN VIRGO

With their analysis and stewing
They accomplish lots of doing.
The wind that really fills their sails
Is to deal with life's details.
Inwardly it gives them thrills
To tackle and pay all the bills.
These are things they need for juice
To make them feel that they're of use.

Though it seems they're so adept,
Deep inside they feel inept.
They're pretty self-effacing
And work hard so they're erasing
All the errors of their lives
(Or their partners', husbands', wives').

And though they will self-criticize
Don't think that they will compromise
On high standards that they hold,
For then they can get very bold.

They're so organized and clean;
They need to work in some routine.
They don't have to be the star
But love to help the ones who are.
They're content to be back stage
Where they more quietly engage.

They're not gushy in affections.
They're good at giving out directions
Be they solicited or not.
They get fussy but not hot.
Their emotions they'll assess
A lot more than they will express.
When first in love they can be shy
But they get through it by and by.
They're happy partners, husbands, wives
When they lead nicely ordered lives.

MOON IN LIBRA

Their responses are genteel
Because they think before they feel.
They fairly easily concede,
All because they have this need
To be the ones who keep the peace
And to help make conflicts cease.

But then on the other hand,
A phrase we know that is their brand,
They can't help it, they see flaws
Which will often be the cause
Of arguments that will arise
When they refuse to compromise
When some injustice has occurred.

There is no way they'll be deterred
From charging right into the fray
To insist they have their say.
Then you may find you're catching hell,
But nicely though—they rarely yell.
They both equivocate and spar.
That's how they find out who they are,
But they do it with such charm
That serves to calm and then disarm.

Whether they are kids or grown
They don't like to be alone.
They just have to socialize
And if they can't part of them dies.
They need to see their tastes reflected,
Like art or people they've collected.

They will often find a mate
In youth who tries to dominate,
But do not stay if they're not fair.
They only want mates who can share.

MOON IN SCORPIO

Their range of feelings is immense
And their responses are intense,
Which of course you'll rarely know
For that's the way of Scorpio.

At times it's really hard to know
Which mood is real or just for show,
So they often gain command
Through means that they have subtly planned.

They may erupt or they may smolder,
And not until they get much older
Do they learn how they can vent
And not have everyone get bent.
If their feelings aren't expressed

Then their bodies get distressed.
For most, in early childhood
Their depths weren't rightly understood.
Their deepest parts were not befriended.
Some of them were not well tended.
There's little that they can't live through
And serve to be our models who
Don't just teach us to survive,
But more importantly to thrive.

Humming like electric wires
Their energies light sparking fires,
Giving them a strange mystique
That makes them people others seek.
But still, they hold themselves apart
And just a few will know their heart.
They're not their best in single lives;
They need partners, husbands, wives.

MOON IN SAGITTARIUS

They do not dwell much on the past
Or whether something's going to last.
It's pretty hard to shock or scare them,
And it can be hard to snare them.
If they need to, they'll confront
And when they do they're pretty blunt.
They're not upset if you get mad.
They'll shrug it off, say, "That's too bad."

Let others seek attention, preening,
These folks need to search for meaning.
Their feelings range to great extremes
Just like the far reach of their dreams.

They like to have it so their earnings
Come from other people's learnings.
They need to take a risk or two
And make some pathways that are new.

They are natural explorers
And are also great abhorrers
Of fences, leashes, things confining.
They have to do their own defining.
They need to travel, have to roam
To places far away from home.
For some their travel is the kind
That broadens knowledge and the mind.

When they're old and wearing dentures
They will still need their adventures.
Even if they don't move much
They still need Mother Nature's touch,
Like doors and windows open wide
Because they like to be outside.
Each must find ways to explore—
That's how they find their inner core.

MOON IN CAPRICORN

They've big emotions to express
But keep their lids on, loathing mess.
The unpredictable they dread,
They need to have a plan instead.
They like conditions well-defined
And people who will act refined.

For most, their mothers figured strongly,
Whether goodly, rightly, wrongly.
Their parents could be nice enough
But somehow couldn't give the stuff
To make these children feel secure.
Many have much to endure.

They're competent and quite efficient.
They're extremely self-sufficient,
So if you offer them assistance
Be prepared to meet resistance.

Their duties they will not forsake,
But they must work on give and take.
At times it feels they don't relate
As much as they officiate.
They need some outlets for release
Or they'll have trouble finding peace.
They don't complain, they don't bemoan,
They just retreat to be alone
But then burst forth with presence large
When there's a need to be in charge.

They aren't the ones who sigh and swoon
While gazing at a big full moon.
They're dependable and steady,
Needing time before they're ready
To commit to say, "I do,"
But once they do they see it through.

MOON IN AQUARIUS

They're a paradox for sure—
Freedom makes them feel secure.
If in love with them you're matched,
Know that they can be detached.
Being loners deep at heart,
They often set themselves apart
Not quite sure if they fit in,
More on the outside looking in.

Since they must express invention,
Most will break from some convention
Regardless of their politics
When there's something they must fix.

Their social conscience is evolved
Which is why they get involved
In every good or half-baked cause
Working hard to change the laws

Which, they fervently explain,
Will make conditions more humane.

When pressure's on they can forget,
Acting like a space cadet.
Their memories are not defective
As much as one could say selective.
For many of them it's their fate
That they will dissociate
From injuries in early years
For which much later come the tears.

They'll listen to most any story,
It matters not how weird or gory.
It's not they like what people say,
They don't know how to get away.

When they are angry, as a rule,
They get distant and are cool.
They don't like people in their face
And give their partners lots of space.
In love they're loyal, though bizarre;
Accept them just for who they are.

MOON IN PISCES

The first thing that is best to mention
Is they don't do well with tension.
They have a hard time saying, "No."
To stand up for themselves they're slow.

Strong emotions find them hurled
Deep within an inner world
Where they retreat to be alone,
Pull down the shades, shut off the phone.

They are compassionate and buffer
Those who feel deep pain and suffer;
Others sympathize in theory,
These folks listen 'til they're bleary.

They are like a psychic sponge
That must be squeezed so they expunge
Emotions, problems others share
With them from aching hearts laid bare.

They have a truly comic sense
And make a real good audience.
They can be very absent-minded,
And at times they can be blinded,
Giving those a warm reception
Whose intention is deception.

They're tenderhearted and they're sweet,
And for their lives to be complete
They do best when they know and feel
They're pledged to serve a high ideal.
Only then, when this is sure
Do they truly feel secure.

Deep within their souls they keep
Many tears they'll never weep.

CHAPTER 4
MERCURY

Mercury is the original multi-tasker. In mythology he is the speediest, busiest, and most versatile of the immortals. Wearing his helmet of invisibility and winged sandals he flies swiftly and unobserved to his many destinations. The role he is most noted for is that of messenger of the gods. In that capacity he carries many secrets which is why in several ancient societies he is revered as the holder and communicator of sacred knowledge, although he is not the source of that knowledge. He has the unique role of being the only immortal able to travel between the land of the living and the land of the dead. Not even Jupiter, king of Olympus, nor Pluto, king of the underworld,* could do this.

Mercury is considered androgynous although he is depicted as male—a young male. There are only scant references to any interest of his in sex and those involve Venus. He mapped out an elaborate and successful contrivance to bed her which, as noted in the chapter on Venus, was not at all difficult. That union produced a child, Hermaphrodites, from which the word hermaphrodite evolved to describe a person with genital characteristics of both genders.

To the ancients the underworld was not what Christianity perceives of as hell, but was the land of the dead, the place everyone went when they died regardless of the quality of their mortal lives.

Movement, cleverness and diversity are Mercury's hallmarks. He is associated with professions that move people, objects or information from one place to another, although he has little interest in the content of what is carried. His acts range from such honored tasks as escorting the newly dead to the underworld, to protecting thieves, to even stealing himself. He can be duplicitous to the point of lying, which is why he has the added designation of Trickster. However, he doesn't usually do these things of his own accord but at the bidding of whatever god commands him.

In his role as messenger, Mercury serves as a connector and mediator. He assisted gods and mortals in their liaisons, sexual and otherwise, also aiding their escape from victimization by others' plotting in those areas. His capacity for bringing one person in contact with another is symbolized by his many associations with pairs: his winged sandals, winged helmet, and his caduceus which is the magical staff he carries, around which twine two serpents and is topped by a pair of wings.

Think how you would act if you could move as he does. What fascinating places you could go, what marvelous discoveries you could make, what innovations you could create, what events you could manipulate, what trouble you could get into. The truth is we all move like that—through our minds.

In astrology Mercury's placement is the indicator of how we use our minds, for our minds are our explorers and connectors. They mediate between our known and unknown worlds, our inner and outer realities, our heavens and hells, and all the disparate elements of our psyches. Sometimes our minds take our bodies along; other times they travel unobserved to where only the imagination can go. Mercury serves many high duties as well as being a mischievous trouble maker, and so do our minds. Just as Mercury is not the source of the sacred knowledge he transmits, neither are our minds the source of our creative animating force. But our minds are what enable us to learn, to use and communicate that knowledge to make sense of our circumstances, to connect with others, to give our lives fullness and meaning.

On a day-to-day level Mercury's astrological placement indicates what information is important to us, how we process information, how we learn, and especially how and what we communicate with others. While the placement of the Sun indicates who we are, Mercury's placement indicates who we say we are. Mercury does not indicate intelligence but shows how we apply the intelligence we have. The sign he is in shows if our mental expressions favor analysis, intuition, investigation, cleverness, strategy, practicality, design or execution of that design. Mercury's special interest in Venus, goddess of love, symbolizes that the mind is always attracted to love. That is a constant.

The placement of Mercury in the astrological chart will never be more than one sign away from the sign your Sun is in.

The fastest and easiest way to find which astrological sign your Mercury is in is to search on the Internet for sites that calculate astrological charts for free. My Mercury is in the sign of _____.

MERCURY IN ARIES

Their speech will tend to be quite often.
There's not much they try to soften;
More than that they are abrupt
And frequently will interrupt.
One can't really call them vicious
Though at times their wit's pernicious
And their irritation can be massive
When dealing with someone who's passive.

They toss their ideas out to catch
And land a hot debating match,
But when others disagree
They are surprised as they can be.
They need to own those conflicts made
When they lob their hand grenade.

They carry light where it is dark
And guide us with their constant spark.
They've endless powers to inspire,
And rarely do they seem to tire
Of kindling all our passion, hopes,
While they ignore the slippery slopes
Of dealing with each dull detail.
They never think that they will fail.

You'll quickly learn these people think
Faster than the eye can blink.
They seem so insurmountable
That few hold them accountable
So they do largely what they please.
Most things come to them with ease,

So if they have to plow through stuff
It drains their energies, it's rough.
They must apply themselves if ever
They will be much more than clever.

MERCURY IN TAURUS

Let others lead the great debate,
These people MUST deliberate.
They have this deep abiding need
To work through process at their speed.
Oh, they can do it fast or slow
But if they don't they will not go.

Just like a plow that tills the ground
Their thinking works best when earthbound.
When they're sorting information
They're colored by how each sensation
Seems to most affect their mood,
Like odor, sound, or tasty food.

They don't get at all bombastic,
But they're surprisingly sarcastic—
Not to cut or wound someone
But just to joke and have some fun.

Because they're practical and placid,
Do not think their minds are flaccid,
And don't consider them as dense.
They're filled with lots of common sense.
Many plans they will reject
Until they know they are correct.
They don't indulge in ideas rash—
Well, maybe, if it brings in cash.

At work or school when each persuades,
They rely on visual aides,
But don't expect they'll be dramatic.
Their style tends to be pragmatic.

It's not that they're not lyrical
They're just so darned empirical.
When they are standing at the helm
They steer us to a realist's realm.

MERCURY IN GEMINI

Their thinking can be so much faster
Than most other folks can master.
They can really entertain
With that over active brain.
Into everything they're peeking
In their constant data seeking.
They are able to extract
Every detail, every fact
From materials they've read
Along with everything that's said.

Their focus will not be sustained
If they're not kept entertained.
They jump from one thing to the next
With speed that makes most feel perplexed.
They'll be text messaging and paging
Other people while engaging
You in active conversation.
It can lead to much frustration.
With their attention often scattered
You may feel you haven't mattered.

If you trap them and they're bored
Then verbally, you may get gored.
They lecture with dexterity
About some faddish verity
Which they just took from avid reading
For their verbal Johnny Appleseeding.

They concoct some brilliant schemes
And have a million plans and dreams,
But their values may diminish

If they don't go on to finish
Clever projects they conceive,
Or else in later life they'll grieve.

MERCURY IN CANCER

Their thinking and their feelings
Interact in all their dealings.
At times they show a talking streak,
Yet other times they do not speak.
They may disappear to brood
When taken over by a mood.

Connected to all that surrounds them,
They take in everything around them.
Their reasoning surpasses fact.
At crucial points before they act
They must seek that place inside them
To intuit what will guide them.

Public speaking makes them shy
In youth, but if they really try,
Which they must do by conscious choice,
Then that will help them find their voice.

They are tactfully evasive
Yet amazingly persuasive.
They rarely are offensive
But are easily defensive,
So prepare yourself, don't be surprised,
They chafe when they are criticized.

You must mine this mother lode
Because they sometimes speak in code,
Sliding off in sideways motion
Like the currents in the ocean.
When they feel they must say more
They might not head straight for the shore
But may just drift about a bit
Before they come right out with it.

MERCURY IN LEO

As sunlight puts blush on the peach
There is great power in their speech.
When they have to charm someone
They pour on warmth, just like the Sun.
They say what others may not dare
And do it with great passion, flair.
They're colorful in all they say
Which often helps them get their way.

They talk to us with real affection
Though they have a predilection
To tell us how things ought to be,
To share with us grand plans they see.
They also get this holy glow
When they can say, "I told you so."

With confidence abounding
Their creativity's astounding.
Our thoughts compare with theirs in scale
As does a minnow to a whale.
They'll dazzle us with all their light
To convince us they are right.

At times they're like an ancient royal
Who thinks an argument's disloyal.
They must learn that their insistence
Often generates resistance,
Which, you see, confuses them
Since what they think enthuses them.

They're gifted how they can disarm
Us with their most magnetic charm,
But if just used for what they please
(Plans to bring them greater ease),
Then they must more than take a peek
Inside to find where they're unique
And use creatively their gift
To give those in their lives a lift.

MERCURY IN VIRGO

They plan things out, they don't just wish.
They view life as their Petri dish,
So we shouldn't be surprised
At ways they have life analyzed.
You will clench both teeth and fists
When they begin compiling lists.

When they approach some brand new topic
They can get real microscopic.
They'll examine all the quirks
So they know how something works.
They're glad to lend a helping hand.
They're at their best when things are planned
As long as they're not pushed or hurried,
Then they can get nervous, worried.

They often say if something fails
Then some one overlooked details,
So they're surprisingly demanding
In the tasks that they're commanding.

They think their minds are their defenses,
Protection from demanding senses.
In youth they underestimate
How passions can make them relate
And lead them to a bad decision
That they never could envision.

They only will recriminate
You if you don't discriminate,
So bluntly telling you the truth.
Take heart, they rarely are uncouth.
Sometimes the detail that each sees
Blocks out the forest for the trees.
They need a principle as guide
So others' views they won't deride.

MERCURY IN LIBRA

You'll notice their loquaciousness
Is nicely laced with graciousness.
When other people get irate
These people rush to moderate.
They'll be diplomatic, subtle
When they offer a rebuttal.

They use feedback as a mirror
To make decision making clearer.
One problem is their need for tact
Can overlook unpleasant fact
Since they don't want to be decisive
If outcomes may be too divisive.
They want conclusions to be nice,
So to that end they give advice.

But don't expect them to maintain
A peace and harmony refrain.
They can see the whole Gestalt
Which they will pick at fault by fault.
It's in their genes—they must compare
One to another, then declare
With every pro there is a con
And then they just go on and on.
Every single factoid counts
As in between the poles they bounce.

Their many words help them in freeing
Up their deeper parts of being,
But first they must find middle ground
For all extremes they know abound.
They can experience deep relief
When finally, they reach belief.

MERCURY IN SCORPIO

Like Sherlock Holmes they will prevail
In digging up each clue, detail,
By probing in your history
To find your hidden mystery.

They will often win first prize
For clever ways they strategize,
How they lay out, plot a course
To trace each problem to its source,
Adept at getting problems solved
(For those with which they're not involved).
Their minds can never truly rest
Until in this they've done their best.

Few, if any, can impeach
Their economy of speech.
They are inclined to buck and balk
At vain attempts to make them talk.
You find instead, it goes to show,
You've told them everything you know;
But if you forge a solid link
Of trust they'll tell you what they think.

Be prepared, they're taciturn,
Quite intense and even stern.
Their searing wit is most succinct
(You might have missed it if you blinked).

Their words cannot identify
The way that they intensify
Their secret little mental notions
That get tangled with emotions.
And don't try to prevaricate,
Embellish, dodge, or obfuscate.
Their mental skills and deep insight
Scope out when something isn't right.

When there's a secret you must tell,
Tell them, they'll keep it very well.

MERCURY IN SAGITTARIUS

They rather like their points of view
Which they are glad to share with you.
Their speech has volume and is blunt
So rarely will you have to hunt
For meaning or for subtlety.
They're subject to hyperbole.

For some the strange or new fatigues
But with these folks it just intrigues.
They are pretty curious
Which tends to make some furious
With all the questions they will ask
While they're pursuing any task.

They learn best when they are hands on.
They won't be anybody's pawn.
They seek out freedom and release
From muzzles by the thought police.

Their organizing is confusing.
What type of system are they using?
Their desks are stacked with lots of stuff
For which there's never time enough
As once a new idea comes in
Their patience for the old runs thin.

They can't help it, they are teachers—
When more zealous, they are preachers.
Although they speak like one anointed
They can sometimes sound disjointed
If a subject's not thought through
And they rush up to speak with you.

They bring the vastness to our reach
By being those who see and teach.
For them it is a thing sublime
To launch another paradigm,
But in pursuit of their high vision

They can sacrifice precision,
And their enthusiasm pales
If they have to give details.

MERCURY IN CAPRICORN

They consider idle chatter
Dumb; to them it doesn't matter.
They have a very structured mind;
If data coming in can't find
Correct and ready storage ports
They'll get pretty out of sorts.

They can be supercilious;
At times they're down right bilious.
They're succinct, no vague conjectures.
They can really give stern lectures.
Being practical and serious
You won't find them too delirious
Over dreams and wild illusions.
These people need some hard conclusions.
They like to know that what they're learning
Can apply to increased earning.

In spite of verbal brevity
They can achieve great levity.
In their responses they transmit
A clever, wry and wicked wit.

They're brilliant how their plans and visions
Come out well with few revisions
Since they are able to complete
A dream from ether to concrete.

They're practical as thinkers,
Plus they have a set of blinkers
Helping keep their vision straight
To only what is on their plate.
Oh, they see dark and they see hell

But don't get stuck and do not dwell
On the failings or the errors
Which bring tragedies and terrors.
Their dilemma—duty calls
That they be there when someone falls.

MERCURY IN AQUARIUS

They don't adhere much to tradition—
They're much more like a first edition.
These people think it's such a blast
To be life's mad iconoclast.
They find it pretty sedentary
Working with the ordinary.

They're eccentric in their views
Which rarely make the evening news
Unless it's fifty years from now
When we won't be here anyhow.
They will relate the unrelated
Be it genius or ill-fated.

Quite detached and scientific
They are painfully specific.
For high tech things they are inclined,
It goes with that electric mind.
They'll talk forever if you let them
(You can stop them if you pet them).

As interested in the chase
As in the victor of the race,
They love to know precisely how
To split an atom, milk a cow,
Exactly how a poem is written,
And where the purr starts in a kitten.

They know so clearly they are right
Each time they get into a fight.
In spite of mixing with the minions

Soaking up diverse opinions,
So surprisingly one finds
They're not inclined to change their minds.

MERCURY IN PISCES

Watching them plot out a course
May make you think they use the Force
Because they use their intuition
Bringing plans into fruition.
They do not judge a lot on acts;
Their perceptions can trump facts.
Their minds work harder on connecting
Than they focus on dissecting.

They don't much need to have their say.
Instead they tend to go away.
They'll dodge and weave if it enhances
Pleasant social circumstances.
They're really clever at evading.
They aren't the strongest in persuading.

They tap archetypal themes
And turn them into dreams or schemes
Done through art or film or words
That can really sway the herds.

Others' thoughts creep in like fog
That steals across a misty bog
And with their own thoughts get infused,
So at times they get confused
As to whom their thoughts belong.
This makes them doubt, think they are wrong.

Their minds will peek behind the veils
To bring us back enchanting tales.
Strong images for them precede
The words that somehow just impede
Expressing thoughts that have their home

Where few of us will ever roam.
As they age it's more compelling
To focus on their inner-dwelling,
Believing there is always more
To be discovered at life's core.

CHAPTER 5
VENUS

Botticelli's famous painting, "The Birth of Venus," greatly sanitized the modern image of Venus, goddess of love, in which she is portrayed as demure and pristine, someone you could take home to mummy for tea as soon as you threw some clothes on her. If the ancient Greeks and Romans weren't already dead they'd die laughing because they knew there was nothing pristine or demure about Venus. In fact, the word "venereal" is derived from her name. It was nearly impossible for any god or mortal to resist or restrain her once her passions were ignited. Jupiter, king of the gods, married her off to the ugly lame god Vulcan and it didn't slow her down one bit.

Venus is goddess of both love and beauty and favors those who value and pursue them. However, she also wants what she wants, so to that end she can be jealous, vindictive, and incredibly manipulative. She is also vain. It was Venus, according to myth, who started the Trojan War by bribing Paris, a poor mortal drafted by Jupiter to judge a beauty contest among the goddesses since no immortal would touch the job. Hers was the best bribe, the most beautiful woman in the world, Helen of Troy, who unfortunately was married to someone else, Menelaus, King of Sparta. But Venus prevailed, Paris got

Helen, Menelaus went ballistic, and the ancient world got a war of such proportions that nearly everyone today has heard at least something about it. All because Venus wanted to win the beauty contest.

The astrological sign Venus is in is the chief indicator of what we want and what we are attracted to. (See the following chapter on Mars for how we go after what we want and how to view Mars and Venus together in your life.) That is why Venus' astrological placement represents what we value since we only value what we would like to have or be. She gives the magnetic power to attract what we want, specific to the characteristics of the sign she is in. She also indicates how we view and experience love relationships as well as the types of social situations we like or don't like.

Venus is the goddess of pleasure with no regrets. She is about desire, not logic. Her birth, according to myth, was from deep in the sea, the kingdom of Neptune representing the unconscious mind. What and who we love and what gives us pleasure are not determined rationally or culturally. These desires come from deep inside us that make us want what we want for no other reason than we want it.

Just because we want something doesn't mean we will get it. Mythology provides a powerful example of this in Venus' unrequited passion for Adonis, a beautiful young mortal. He repeatedly rejected her, so in exasperation she kidnapped him. During his captivity she brought her best game, all her seductive powers full force on him and for the goddess of love that is a lot! All she succeeded in doing was to toughen his resistance. He would rather hunt with his buddies than sleep with her—quite an insult. Eventually admitting defeat she released Adonis, though still obsessed. She followed him to the hunt, where horrified she witnessed him fatally gored by a wild boar. Even the gods do not always have the power to get what they want.

Venus is the giver of gifts of love, as well as little gifts such as jewelry, sweet treats, and small sums of money. This is why the ancients referred to her as "the Lesser Benefic." Jupiter is the giver of larger types of gifts. Venus had no trouble accepting gifts. In fact she expected and often demanded them. After all, her husband was not only the smith of the gods, he was their jeweler and lavished his wife with many of his exquisitely crafted adornments. She found this the upside of her arranged marriage to him.

Many of the myths about Venus center on her love life, specifically the sexual side of it, but she is a great deal more than just a drop-dead gorgeous face and body with a siren-like irresistible allure. We sell her short to only concentrate on her pleasure aspects although she makes it clear that pleasure is not to be denied her or, by extension, us. She consoles the heartbroken. She also tests lovers, forcing them to demonstrate the strength and endurance of their love for their beloveds.

Even though our love lives may occupy a lot of our imaginations, in day-to-day living we spend the majority of our time concentrating on other things. Likewise, the verses about Venus focus more on her day-to-day expressions, specific to the sign she is in.

The placement of Venus in the astrological chart won't be more than two signs away from your Sun sign.

The fastest and easiest way to find which astrological sign your Venus is in is to search on the Internet for sites that calculate astrological charts for free. My Venus is in the sign of _____.

VENUS IN ARIES

What they want they want it now.
They're real clever as to how
They get people to commit
By using their great charm and wit.
They always find ways to have fun
And they'll spend time with anyone
Unless they find them boring—
Then off they go exploring.

When they play they play real hard,
Kind of like a St. Bernard.
When they like you, you will know it.
Enthusiastically they show it.
They're charming as expressers
Which can mask that they're aggressors.
Male and female both compete
For each new lover that they meet.
They really get off on the chase;
They treat each contest as a race.

They rarely show a tendency
To display much codependency,

And they can almost start a war
When others' views they flat ignore.
With age they learn not to deride
And work on their receptive side.

They develop their own style.
They are incapable of guile
So they don't censor what they say.
Still, people like them anyway.
They want to be more than they are
And aspire to go far,
But not in ways the masses think;
They like to be at some new brink.

VENUS IN TAURUS

The style in which they like to live
Is gracious and conservative.
They like the nice things that life offers,
So they work to fill their coffers.

They like luxuries and treats
And are very fond of sweets.
Does it matter, would it hurt
To have seconds on dessert?
Their loved ones have to look real sharp
And if they don't then they will harp
On how they really could look better
If they'd wear a different sweater.

A warm and caring loving friend,
They will support you and defend
You from all slings and arrows cast.
Be assured their friendships last.

One key to them, of course, is
Their stockpiling of resources.
Industrious, hardworking, yet
They are inclined to get in debt.

Resisting impulse is so hard,
They just whip out the credit card.
Their love of pleasure's in their blood.
They roll in it like pigs in mud,
But they must plan their gaiety
Which hampers spontaneity.
They're not that temped to carouse.
They aren't the quickest to arouse,
So if you want a love sublime
Be sure to give them lots of time;
But once you light their passion's fire
It burns steady, they don't tire.

VENUS IN GEMINI

Venus placed in Gemini
Needs constant social stimuli.
Their social networks are extended
To anyone they have befriended.

They like to be an active dater
And may prefer commitment later.
These people really like to flirt
And are surprised that it can hurt.

Informed on all the latest news
They socialize with whom they choose
Since they're not guided by tradition.
They want to act, not seek permission.
They crave and seek variety
And might ignore propriety
With all those choices to explore.
They find restrictions quite a bore.

They move through life with lots of speed,
They like best those who like to read.
They're less concerned about your looks
Than in the content of your books,
Because in matters of the heart

They want a lover who is smart.
The greatest love affairs they find
Are with those who use their mind,
So people they will be inviting
Are stimulating and exciting.

The quickest way that you can prove
Your love to them is on the move.

VENUS IN CANCER

The past for them yields lots of treasure;
To study it brings them much pleasure.
They like to learn of old traditions
Browsing through rare old editions.

They like talking over food.
For them it helps to set the mood,
So if you want their hearts to steal
Provide them a fantastic meal.

They value contacts that are deep;
Those are relationships they keep.
They're deeply sensitive and caring
And most generously sharing
In all forms of their relating,
Not just the ones that lead to mating.
Sensitive to others' needs
They quietly will do good deeds.

So like a calm and glassy sea,
Their outsides make it hard to see
Strong currents moving far below,
But as you plumb their depths you'll know.
At times they hide, like crabs in sand;
It's best that loved ones understand
Their inner states must take a rest
So they can do their very best.

When in love once they are ready
To commit then they'll be steady.
They're sensuous in their expression
Which can cause guilt and repression;
Commitment makes them feel secure.
There's much from loved one's they'll endure.
They may travel, they may roam,
But they need family, they need home.

VENUS IN LEO

As soon as these folks leave the womb
They know how to fill a room.
It doesn't matter where they are,
At work, the gym—they are a star.
They hope their entrances are grand:
"What, no flowers? Where's the band?"

They have a great ability
To radiate nobility.
They have a flair for the dramatic
And people find them charismatic.
Their unique flamboyant style
Puts some off, makes others smile.

They're generous and like to share
Themselves, but loved ones be aware
They do it reigning from a throne
And like to rule there all alone.

They are indeed an earthly treasure
When enjoying some fond pleasure,
But can unsheathe some sharpened claws
Hidden in their gentle paws.
Oh, they can put on quite a show
When disagreed with or told, "No."
When they sense they're not adored
They pout or sulk or act real bored.

The men all think that they're Lord Byrons.
Women? They're Ulysses' Sirens.
At least that is the working stance
With which they both approach romance.
Remember this and be alert,
As they will often boldly flirt.

As they age they see the mirror
Held by life that makes much clearer
Their potential there to see,
Their gift to others they can be.

VENUS IN VIRGO

Hard workers, they're the people who
Like tasks that no one wants to do.
They aren't wooed by fame or perqs;
They just want to do good works.

Both an analyst and thinker
They can't help it, they must tinker
With all systems, structures, orders.
They like to redraw all old borders,
But if their efforts are refused
Then they tend to get confused.

They'll help to bolster up the team,
But when it comes to self-esteem
They lean toward feeling they've a dearth
Of confidence and strong self-worth.

Even in their early youth
They're repelled by things uncouth.
As lovers they're detailed, efficient;
Few will feel that they're deficient.
In close encounters of the heart
They often get a rocky start.
When it comes to choosing mates
They rarely leave much to the Fates,

Looking under all the covers
Of potential partners, lovers
Searching for each flaw, defect
Their love can change, perhaps perfect.
In double harness they endure
Which gives them time to find a cure.

With this placement don't forget,
They really like to have a pet.

VENUS IN LIBRA

These folks are just so gosh darned nice
Even when they give advice.
They love to go to different places;
They're versed in all the social graces
Knowing how we all should be
At stock car races or high tea,
Which maximizes social traction
When engaged in interaction.
But in their need to be so pleasing
They can go overboard appeasing.

They are among the few quite able
To bring all parties to the table
Helping them to interact
To keep relationships intact.

They're gracious and they like to share.
They don't like people who aren't fair.
They have high standards and prefer
To be with those who won't incur
Embarrassment from some crass act.
Mostly they're a real class act.

They need harmony and balance—
Curtains have to match the valance.
They might get unbalanced, though
If their surroundings aren't just so.

The thought of love, not its hot fire,
Is what stimulates desire.
Although they talk to everyone,
They need that special one on one.

VENUS IN SCORPIO

Flowers do not chase the bees.
These are people more at ease
With being those who stand and wait
To let their magic captivate.
Some of them say it's debasing
To be the ones to do much chasing.

They hum and glow with sex appeal.
Their magnetism makes you reel.
If not so, they seem good looking,
All the better, dear, for hooking
You their object of desire.
Oh, they can really stoke that fire.
Be careful here, make no mistake—
They'll charm the skin right off a snake.

When they're forced to socialize
They'll look quite deeply in your eyes
Searching for your strengths and faults,
Your raw potential, treasure vaults.
They like what they can only see
By using depth psychology,
Probing, getting you to tell
Your secret heaven, private hell.

Often they will act removed
Until somehow (don't ask) you've proved
That you have something way down deep
That might be valuable to keep.

They'll treat you just like royalty
Once you've proved your loyalty.

But there is something you should know—
In love they like to run the show.

VENUS IN SAGITTARIUS

They love to talk philosophy,
Big codes and laws—how we should be.
Still, they don't like to be confined
By rules that make them act refined.
Oh, they can do the social graces
But they prefer to be in places
Where they feel that they are free
To be and act most naturally.

Their pleasure appetites are hearty;
A bacchanal is how they party.
Marriage anarchists are they
When young, but most don't stay that way.
They can live with love that's strained
As long as they are entertained.
They tolerate a lot of stuff
If their leash is long enough.

They strongly value the ideal,
For it's as tangible, as real
As any money in the bank
Or station, office held, or rank.
For cares of life they seek relief
By searching out a new belief.

They really like and find appealing
When others share what they are feeling.
You need not fear their repercussions;
It's all good fuel for great discussions.

Throughout their lives this is a must—
To be their friend you must be just.
And if you want to be the one
To run with them, you must be fun.

To be their partner, husband, wife
Be hopelessly in love with life.

VENUS IN CAPRICORN

They like people who are old.
They don't warm up until they're sold
That they can trust that you will act
So reputations stay intact.
If you want to win their heart
It helps if you look good, are smart,
So you may find you need their clearance
When it comes to your appearance.

Even when they've strong attractions
They can be stiff in interactions.
They won't tell you that, here's why—
They tend to be a little shy.

From the moment of their birth
They have to know what is their worth.
They can shelve their wants and needs
To concentrate upon those deeds
Calculated to enhance
Conditions that help them advance.

Deep down they're romantic souls,
With lots of plans for reaching goals.
They're flustered by folks who are gushy
So out in public don't get mushy.
They're not at ease with letting go
When strong emotions start to flow,
But be assured their passion's there
Which in commitment they best share.

They have patience and can wait
A long time for that perfect mate.
Their faithfulness will rarely falter
Once you get them to the alter,

But rapport just may turn sour
If they cannot share in power.

VENUS IN AQUARIUS

The course to their desires steered
May seem to others just plain weird,
Since what they value, don't forget,
Hasn't been invented yet.

They're quick to recognize a trend
And will brightly recommend
Reasons why you should pursue it
And clever ways that you can do it.

They are the ones who like to shatter
Concepts that no longer matter,
So they find doctrine so confining
And will work at redesigning
All of culture's shackling laws
To help to rid us of those flaws.

Their eyes beneath unruly hair
Will have a tendency to stare
And don't reveal how things will end–
As a lover or a friend.
If they get to have their druthers,
We'd love all our sisters, brothers
As long as it is done in groups,
Teaching, firing up the troops.

They'd rather be just friends than lovers
But hold their own beneath the covers.
If lovers start to think long term
Then it tends to make them squirm,
But when love strikes them, it hits hard
And hoists them on their own petard.
This bond of love lasts them forever,
A bond no knives can ever sever.

VENUS IN PISCES

They believe that life's a whole
And chafe at those who must control
Through use of dogma which decreases
Unity it cuts in pieces.

They love tales of fairies, elves
In which they seek to lose themselves.
They're tuned to songs the angels sing
And visions that they often bring,
And you will be amazed and swear
That they pull poems straight from the air.

They wonder if they render less
From ecstasy than tenderness,
A question others rarely ask—
It seems to be their cosmic task.

To those in pain they're tender, nice
And for them they will sacrifice
Their time and lots of energy,
And for that they won't charge a fee.

They seem to do best with a mate
Who will let them isolate.
If you want to be their honey
They don't care if you have money.
It's easy for them to believe,
Which makes them easy to deceive.

They love more deeply than they tell,
So love affairs can cause them hell
As early on they fall for dopes
And then their lives turn into Soaps.
Eventually they do get wise
And learn to see with inner eyes.

CHAPTER 6
MARS

Mars is best known as the god of war. No god was his equal in battle. In earlier mythology he was the god of spring, fertility and new growth. What links these two roles is that Mars creates new forms by breaking down old ones. Much is destroyed in the carnage of war. Governments topple, cities crumble, people die. Newness always follows that could not emerge without the rapid decimation caused by war, just as in spring new life emerges from the death of winter. No life in the plant or animal kingdoms can occur without fertilization, again the sphere of Mars. Mythology shows us that he makes numerous contributions in that department, especially to Venus.

Just as Venus is the astrological indicator of what we want, Mars shows us how we go after what we want. As with Venus, Mars doesn't care if what or who we want inconveniently belongs to someone else, or doesn't want us back. These two are perfectly matched. Their desires are from deep in the psyche symbolized by the fact that their love affair was outside marriage, beyond the bounds of what is accepted in and regulated by civilization. People and situations we crave or that seem to crave us are not dictated or even moderated by what others consider moral or proper. Throughout history, no laws, no norms, no pulpit-pounding preaching have been able to stop these desires when they surge, just as no one could keep Mars and Venus apart if they wanted to be together.

One of the many myths about their passionate liasons describes when Vulcan, Venus' husband, was angered at repeatedly being cuckolded by Mars—and in his own marriage bed. Since he was jeweler and smith of the gods, he crafted an invisible net of chains so strong yet so fine that no one, including another immortal, could see it. He placed it in his marriage bed to catch the two of them in the act. Sure enough his trap worked and snared the unsuspecting lovers. Vulcan triumphantly summoned all the deities to join him in witnessing the shame of these two. Only that isn't quite how it came off. For starters, none of the goddesses came, only gods. At first they laughed at invincible Mars caught in lame Vulcan's clever trap, but their mood soon shifted to envy. They started talking among themselves, locker room conversations, and Apollo even asked Mercury, the least likely of the immortals to be sexually interested in anyone, if he would mind being caught in the net of chains for the chance to sleep with Venus. Mercury replied that even if there were three times as many chains, and even if all the gods were looking on, he would indeed love to have that opportunity. Then Neptune, god of the sea symbolizing the unconscious mind, told Vulcan to free them, but Vulcan demanded restitution from Mars as compensation for his damaged reputation and ego. It appeared that no one really expected Mars to pay up, so Neptune said he would. Vulcan agreed and Mars got off without paying. The two lovers were released, each running off to a different exotic island, each appearing completely unchastened.

Initially it seems that Mars and Venus got off without paying any restitution, but the fact that Neptune made that payment indicates that the unconscious pays the price and will demand payment somewhere down the road when least expected. Also, such unions produce children even if only in a symbolic sense. Mars and Venus had children together, out of wedlock, of course: Phobos, meaning fear, Deimos, meaning panic or terror, and Harmonia, meaning harmony—names that describe the possibilities resulting from such unions. Phobos and Deimos some will recognize as the names astronomers gave the two moons of the planet Mars. Some myths say that Eros, god of love, was also their child.

In astrology, Mars represents the aggressive, instinctive, angry and often uncivilized parts of our nature, which is why the ancients referred to him as the "Lesser Malefic." (Saturn was the "Greater Malefic.") Mars does not sit in contemplation with his feet before the fire. He *is* the fire. He has to be on the move. Modern times provide few outlets for Mars to give full range to his energy, passion and aggression. How he moves is indicated by the astrological sign this warrior occupies, how we achieve our individual desires, also how we defend ourselves when attacked. Do we bob and weave or roar out of the chute like a surface-to-air missile, or do we launch the sneakier torpedo? With conflicts, do we cause them, mediate them or simply walk away from the battlefield? Is our energy forcefully channeled or do we run out of steam? The armor Mars wears is influenced again by sign. Does he wear a three-piece pinstripe suit to storm the board rooms, the unobtrusive look of a private investigator, an athlete's uniform, a techno-weenie's nerdy attire?

Clearly, Mars and Venus are a pair, but remember, not a pair sanctioned by civil laws. Their energies are more like two freight trains crashing into each other. Therefore, it's important to take a good look at the placements of Venus and Mars in our charts to determine if they complement each other or conflict. It's usually some combination. In this evaluation keep in mind the key concepts for each: Venus indicates what we want, what we value, and what we seem to attract, and Mars indicates what we go after and how we do it.

Following are some scenarios for someone with Venus in Pisces and Mars in Capricorn. As the verses indicate, someone with Venus in Pisces values selfless acts, the betterment of others and the alleviation of suffering. Mars in Capricorn will have an itch for ambition that will not be scratched by anything except achievement. There is potential for these energies to work well together, like if the person decides to take a leadership position in an organization with a humanitarian focus. However, if the drive is to succeed on Wall Street or in the board room, then the person can have uncomfortable inner conflicts demanding attention.

Regardless of where Mars is in our charts, he will be our instrument for bringing something new through our psyches and into the world. In that process not everything that was there before will remain standing, nor should it. Perhaps we would be more tolerant of intensely burning desires and passions in ourselves and others if we viewed them less as coming from the personality and more from deep in life itself, making us restless, pushing us to move into the uncharted territories that will become the landscapes of our futures.

The fastest and easiest way to find which astrological sign your Mars is in is to search on the Internet for sites that calculate astrological charts for free. My Mars is in the sign of _____.

MARS IN ARIES

Propelled by constant inner fire
(And they mistake this for desire),
They have a strong compelling need
To blaze through life at daunting speed,
Acting much like they're Top Guns,
Approaching life as bombing runs.

Their instincts are what guide their acts
More than strategy and facts.
They crave action so they need
To be the ones who take the lead.
If they fail they don't despair,
They say, "I guess it wasn't there,"
And quickly turn and set their sights
On other unachieved great heights.

They don't try to set a mood
And sometimes can be downright rude.
All this energy they've got
Can discharge like a rifle shot.
Their flare-ups happen pretty fast.
Take heart—they leave them in the past.
They work best when a project's new
As they get bored with follow-through.
In everything they do or say
Is genius geared to get their way.
Detractors quickly they disarm
By changing energy to charm.

They cannot truly be constrained,
Just temporarily detained.
Mostly they're a step ahead;
They've two speeds only—fast and dead.
You'll hear them say, "I'll slow down now."
The truth is, though, they don't know how.

MARS IN TAURUS

They may not be first in the chase
But they'll win the endurance race.
Rarely will you call them quitter.
Not blinded by bright flash or glitter,
They will work hard to assure
The goals they reach make them secure
Which likely they will realize
Since they can plan and organize.

Their tempers only are invoked
When they have really been provoked.
They're stable and don't get real jangled.
You won't find them all entangled
In the dramas of the day,
Like how things shift and move and sway.
They will navigate resistance
With unfaltering insistence
To stay the course and not change tack.
Few things pull them off the track.

But when they're stoking up the fires
Of their personal desires,
They may miss the subtle signs
That something's wrong with their designs.
They need to set time to assess
That they're not heading for some mess.

No rocket is their Taurus Mars,
And yet they'll take you to the stars.
You'll go first class, they'll plan it well.
When you arrive you'll rest a spell
Before you roll in fields of flowers
Which they do expertly for hours.

MARS IN GEMINI

Lack of movement tires them.
Lots of choice inspires them.
Their quick movements seem erratic.
It's just that they don't like things static.
They can't be still for very long
And wander where they don't belong.
The work in which they do their best
Is that which keeps their interest.
They're proud of their quite nimble speed
And few are warnings that they heed.
Their words and actions are so fast;
Relationships don't always last.
They'll talk a blue streak in your face
With minds gone to another place.
Being restless, curious souls
They can handle many roles.
Let others hold and wield the gavel,
They would rather move and travel.

It's hard to do but you can try,
To beat Mars' wit in Gemini.
Yes, they're funny, this is true
And even more, they think so too.
The last one any would call dunce,
They can read three books at once.
They seem to manage to succeed
At juggling tasks with break-neck speed.

If for their actions they're berated
They can get real irritated.
Their anger has to be expressed
With words or their minds get real messed,
And as they age they need to learn
To do that without acid burn.

MARS IN CANCER

Mars in Cancer can melt ice,
When in a mood to act real nice.
Passion runs through them like tides,
Surges strongly then subsides.

You never know how they'll display
Their anger, what they'll do or say.
They'll be like crabs down on the beach
Who dig a hole, hide out of reach.
Other times they'll puff up, fight
When they've sustained some minor slight.
They need to get things out, assert,
Or else their stomachs start to hurt.

They have pitches so compelling
When engaged in forms of selling;
They can quickly spot a trend,
When it will start, where it will end.

They have a plan that's in their mind.
It's detailed, clear, and then they find
The path they take does not go straight—
They circle, sidestep, deviate.
But once they get there they do well
Though they can put themselves through hell.

They're sensuous and show their caring
By their nurturing and sharing
Unless they're moody, feeling needy;
Then they can get kind of greedy.
They have a therapeutic zeal
And like it when they help or heal.

MARS IN LEO

They are direct and quite emphatic
With a flair for the dramatic.
They like to be those who engage
Their energies on some big stage,
Like off to Vegas to throw dice
Or skiing slopes of snow and ice,
Or launching concepts bold and new
Far ahead of current view.

When they get blocked they can surprise
You with the ways they'll improvise.
They have a goodly share of talent,
Not real humble but they're gallant.
Telling them what you admire
About them fuels their inner fire.
Playful as the lion cubs
They rarely ever use their clubs
Unless they feel attention due
Is way too slow in coming through.

They're kindly when in leadership
Unless they're on an ego trip.
They're warriors cloaked in royalty,
So they expect some loyalty
As when they have to work in groups.
They want support from all the troops.
It's best if others understand
They really are a one man band.

Their matters of the heart advance
With heavy doses of romance,
Accoutrements that they require
To fuel and keep alive desire.

They need to learn at intersections
When they have to choose directions,
That they must choose what really matters,
Though they're drawn to that which flatters.

MARS IN VIRGO

Mars in Virgo shows reserve,
It keeps them focused, helps them serve.
Even though they like to serve us
Way deep down they can get nervous
That no matter what their stuff
Somehow it's never good enough.

They're helpful for the asking
And they're great at multi-tasking.
When they act they are discrete.
Their inspirations are concrete.
You will find them quite resourceful
In their work, though not too forceful.
But if you do not show respect
For their systems they object
And get defensive, start to harp.
That's when their anger can get sharp.

When it's time to run the race
They'll cheer you on from second place;
For them it's not to get there first
But on the way there be well versed.

Their full detailed analysis
Can lead to near paralysis,
We wish (a little) they'd neglect
Their urge just to perfect, perfect!
But they are so defendable
Because they're so dependable.

Great stewards of the public trust,
Ensuring details are discussed
They work to see that those involved
Heal the problems to be solved.

MARS IN LIBRA

They get angry graciously
And rarely act rapaciously.
Like fists soft wrapped in velvet gloves
They're warriors trapped in peaceful doves.
While others go forth with war cries
They reach out trying to find allies,
Yet they will get us to compete
In games to lead us to defeat.

They love arguments, debate
Which they most passionately state,
But they will stop just short of fighting
Even when injustice righting,
For they must balance all aggression
With harmonious expression.
They'll get things done, but often late
Because they will procrastinate.
What they're really masters of
Is seeing beauty, touting love,
But mood and lighting must be right
Before their passion fires light.

They need relationships as anchor
Though they may be filled with rancor
Because they're drawn to fires made
By those who throw the hand grenade.
When conflicts start they don't deny it—
But say they start it? They don't buy it.
This is what they have to learn,
When fires rage they've helped them burn.

MARS IN SCORPIO

They have this great propensity
For deeply felt intensity
Both in themselves and others, hence,
Their partners, too, are quite intense.

They charm and dazzle all they know
While they dig to look below.
Those who work with them have found
They do their best work underground.
They keep their lids on, as a rule
And rarely ever lose their cool,
But if they do you'd better hide—
You may get torched, or worse, freeze-dried.

Their passion is quite physical.
They're relentless how they're quizzical.
Detectives of the zodiac,
There isn't much you can hold back
Even if you're trying.
They have their ways of prying.

They see what other people don't,
And they may do what others won't.
Regarding options when they choose,
They're not concerned about taboos.
They'll sense and sniff out all things hidden
And often seek what is forbidden.

They're daunting when they are a foe,
Although, at first, it's hard to know
Because they'll take a lot of flack
Before they expertly fight back.

Because they are so darned intense
They have to have an inner fence
That separates their fiery passion
From their need for cold dispassion.
That's why they can run cold or hot,
Why they do nothing or a lot.

MARS IN SAGITTARIUS

Their fingers are in lots of pies.
They may not take time to apprise
Themselves and others, risks involved
And other problems to be solved.
Though they can plan they may eschew it
Because if it feels good they do it.

They love to contemplate the stars
While driving in their sporty cars,
Or trail bike, pack horse, or canoe—
Any transport type will do…
…Or exercise their mental states
Through long discussions or debates.

That which turns them on with zeal
Is following some truth, ideal,
But they can run a bit rough shod
Proclaiming their belief or god.
Then they're surprised by opposition
Others take to their position.
So you'll often get an earful,
But thankfully they're pretty cheerful.

Their logic sometimes skips some beats.
They lean more toward the daring feats.
They'll move around in their employment
Seeking jobs where there's enjoyment.
Their playfulness must have its run.
These people die if there's no fun.

They roam the corners of the earth
And live far from their place of birth.
They have to risk, they have to strive.
That's how they know that they're alive.

MARS IN CAPRICORN

They think hard work is something good,
A concept learned in childhood.
Their ambitions are quite large
And they're so good at being in charge,
Often called upon to lead
Since others know they will succeed.

Some with Mars in Capricorn
Aspire to the manner born.
Achievement, power may inspire
Them to reach their heart's desire.
They can martial all their forces
Helping them to set their courses.

A plough horse who will win the race,
They don't obviously chase.
They're disciplined how they pursue
Their goals and how they see things through.
Their outcomes are extraordinary.
They know how to thrust and parry
At any trying to control
Or limit progress to their goal.
It's not enough that they have tried,
They do not want success denied.

Whether homemakers or lawyers
They can act like Spartan warriors,
And though they can seem so controlled
Don't ever think that they are cold.
The ways that they stoke passion's flame
Can put a Scorpio to shame.

They're able to potentiate
Their self-expression to be great.
Their challenge is can they attain
Great heights, but not cause others pain.

MARS IN AQUARIUS

A brilliant prophet, funny clown,
They either break through or break down.
They've a wit hilarious
Though sometimes deleterious.

They love to poke and rearrange
And move things for the sake of change.
Whatever new plan they have hatched
They'll put in motion so detached
You may not catch on right away
That they are paving some new way.

They let others live life free
Because that's how they want to be.
They don't get up in your face
Because they, too, need lots of space.

They don't just want to have their say
They also want to have their way,
So don't ignore their stubborn streak.
The things they do will be unique.
They act just for the hell of it
And then they think quite well of it.

They cannot be one of the herd.
They think there's nothing too absurd
Or offbeat, nuts, or too inane
If it might make life more humane.
But whatever their endeavor
It must be new, it must be clever.

They'll be culture's great physicians
Or just clever stage magicians.

MARS IN PISCES

Lots of action makes them wilt,
Strong emotions give them guilt.
Often they'll just let things go,
Easier to ride the flow.
Then their focus tends to shift
And these are times they seem to drift.
As flexible as rubber bands
They can have trouble taking stands.

They have a helpful attitude.
Their acts inspire gratitude.
They do their best work when they heed
The call of those in pain or need.
How many of them do their parts
Is through the work of healing arts.
They have great proclivity
For amazing creativity
Which they can brilliantly display
On stage or screen or cabaret.

They have a tendency to brood
But do a lot when in the mood.
Like meteors that hit the sea
They can lose their energy.
They're not planners, they intuit
Everything before they do it.

They must join with feeling mates
And are concerned with inner states.
They're motivated by their visions
Which serve to help them make decisions.
They work from faith small as a seed.
They're not inflamed by power, greed
But by the good that they can do.
They may need help to see it through.

CHAPTER 7
JUPITER

In the genealogy of the gods Jupiter was born into the third generation which traditionally starts to bring respectability to a family whose progenitors have not behaved well. Jupiter's grandparents, Ouranos and Gaia, were king and queen of the Titans or First Gods, and were the "Adam and Eve" of ancient Greek and Roman mythology. Ouranos was so tyrannical that his wife urged their son Saturn (Jupiter's father) to kill Ouranos which he does by castrating him. It gets worse. Later Saturn ate all of his children except Jupiter, but it doesn't come out as badly as it first seems. Jupiter did eventually overthrow his father, but nipping a bad family tradition in the bud, did so without killing him, demonstrating that while the apple doesn't fall far from the tree it certainly can roll some distance from it. Furthermore, he tricked his father into regurgitating back to life all the children he swallowed. There is a mythic and astrological significance for this which will be discussed in the following chapter on Saturn.

Jupiter was first known as the sky or storm god with an arsenal of thunderbolts. He became king of the heavens and the earth, father god of all living beings. In fact, many pictoral representations of God in the Judeo-Christian traditions are based on earlier depictions of Jupiter. Jupiter was also father god in other ways, to the aggravation of his wife, Juno. He is credited with fathering more offspring than any other god, and mostly not with Juno.

As head of the government of the gods he was the great convener, calling everyone together when there was a problem to address. These assemblies seldom produced tangible results, but that wasn't the point. The point was that the inadequacies of the old ways had to be acknowledged and addressed so a new concept could emerge. When the gods are involved in creation it is chaotic and messy. If the dynamics of the conclave got too far out of hand as was usually the case, like a judge presiding over a trial, Jupiter kept things moving. How this occurred wasn't his first priority. Details took a back seat to progress, a key point to remember about Jupiter.

While Jupiter was the great convener, he was not the great decider. When faced with a particularly difficult problem he'd often grab some mortal and force him or her, as only a god can do, to make a decision the gods didn't want to make. The gods could act a lot like Congress. They wanted to be liked by us mortals so they tended to shy away from tough calls for fear of negative publicity, looking for a convenient scapegoat. Mortals were the perfect scapegoats because the gods outranked them. Plus they were easily manipulated, as those drafted for these tasks suddenly found themselves in the intoxicatingly seductive company of deities. In this inflated state it was nearly impossible for them to realize that they were in over their heads, unable to foresee the disaster sure to follow that would have only their fingerprints all over it, such as the start of the Trojan War described in the Venus chapter.

The sign Jupiter is in indicates how we find wisdom through the possibilities that lay outside the heavy curtains of rules and fear drawn around our lives. He also represents how intoxicating those possibilities can feel. He fills us with confidence, sometime over-confidence, so that we not only want to part those curtains, we also feel that everything is in place to do so. We make that risky move, take that leap of faith, and chase that big dream because it seems so right at the time. How else could we break out? Sometimes—a lot of times—it pays off. Sometimes it doesn't, but with Jupiter we always think it will.

Jupiter is the good guy of the zodiac, referred to by the ancients as the "Greater Benefic." He was known for his exceptional generosity in bringing gifts and rewards, chiefly fame and fortune which could strike like one of his lightning bolts. In ancient times there were only two ways of obtaining fortune, to be born into it or have it bestowed by the gods, namely Jupiter. In modern times our concept of fortune is more related to the potential for earnings from one's career or sheer dumb luck. Therefore, Jupiter is today a chief astrological indicator of potential in one's professional life, although he still remains ruler of the "striking out of the blue" type of luck.

No matter what happens, we learn something from a Jupiter experience. Since learning is also the result of formal education, the placement of Jupiter in the chart also indicates what our educational environment may be, and what forces shape it. Jupiter's true goal is for us to find increased knowledge and wisdom that only the journey can bring. It is in the human condition that we find wisdom through experience which can be about gaining material riches, prominence, or enlightenment and what happens to us when we do or do not find them.

Jupiter rules laws and social order, particularly the vision and purpose behind those laws. He is about the spirit of the law while his father, Saturn, is about the letter of the law. Jupiter and Saturn have a carrot and stick relationship, with Jupiter the enticing carrot and Saturn the parental stick, even though they both have the same purpose—different methods—of moving us into finding out who we are. How these two planets relate to each other in your chart will be explored in the Saturn chapter to follow.

Everything about Jupiter is large. He is the most robust god in size. He has the greatest responsibility. He has the loudest voice. He has such powers that he can elevate anyone to immortality as a constellation in the heavens. It is no coincidence that the largest planet in our solar system is named for him.

The highest expression of Jupiter in the astrological chart is the expansion of consciousness, so the sign Jupiter is in indicates the area of life in which this will be focused, though by no means confined to it. Sometimes this expansion can lead to inflation and overconfidence, the consequences of which also produce lessons in consciousness.

Jupiter indicates how we seek and come to know deity personally, not the deity others think we should have. The message of Jupiter, wherever he is in our charts, is to go with confidence and generosity into the future, filled with faith that there is bounty and goodness and purpose in life.

Jupiter spends one year in each sign. Therefore, he is the first generational astrological marker of traits you will share with many of those your own age. His placement in the astrological chart indicates not only the personal aspects described in this section but an expanded consciousness of social connectedness, a need to become aware of broader issues and themes.

The fastest and easiest way to find which astrological sign your Jupiter is in is to search on the Internet for sites that calculate astrological charts for free. My Jupiter is in the sign of _____.

JUPITER IN ARIES

They're pretty self-reliant
And deceptively defiant.
Those engaged in formal training
Often find it dull and draining.
Even though they see it through
They learn most from the things they do.

They grow by blazing some new trail.
Their value isn't did they fail
But did it hasten their expanding
Of their state of understanding.

A principle to them that's key—
They must maintain integrity
Because if someone can't be true
To self, what matters what they do?

When they're blocked they rarely whine.
Most structures they will redefine.
If work place rules make them annoyed
They may walk out unemployed.

They're energetic pioneers
Who get as many jeers as cheers.
And through the years as they get older
Experience just makes them bolder.
They find their god and who they are
By following a lonely star.

JUPITER IN TAURUS

They have voices folks obey.
They're convincing and can sway
People's views in ways compelling,
So they're very good at selling.

Their outcomes can't be realized
Until completely visualized.
They do the most when they are able
To keep foundations strong and stable.
They will seek and find resources
To help them plod their well planned courses.
The best way that they grow, improve
Is working in a steady groove.

They're magical with new things growing,
Coming from instincts of knowing
How we best can "till the fields"
In ways that can increas all yields.

Not much given to pretenses,
They take life in through all their senses.
If in youth they lacked affection,
This may give a predilection
That they search for life's deep treasures
In possessions, sensate pleasures.
It's their tendency to cling
To comfort that things worldly bring,
But they won't say that they're averse
To seek depth in the universe.
In time they will accept that place
Where human coarseness binds with grace.

JUPITER IN GEMINI

Their deity is information;
Their chariot—communication.
They value all of life's good teachers
But do not think much of those preachers
Who use doctrine as mind shackles.
That can really raise their hackles,
So they may chafe at discipline
That seeks to rein their focus in.

They think ideas should be discussed,
Debate and argument's a must.
They'll find academics boring
If they're prevented from exploring.
They find a way to keep things moving
Without going for approving.

Each new thought has great appeal
And they pursue each one with zeal,
But when they make each new connection
They need to pause for deep reflection.

It's important, when they're young,
That someone guides their mind and tongue
To not hastily just blurt
Out those things that can cause hurt.

Many choices they can see
To use to meet their destiny,
But any path they choose to enter
Should somehow lead back to their center.

JUPITER IN CANCER

Many of them flourish
In professions geared to nourish.
What really makes them feel secure
Is working hard so they ensure
That others get help with survival.
That gives them spiritual revival.

If when young they could depend
On loved ones, then they can extend
Their awareness so they see
That mankind is their family.
But if in youth needs are ignored
They can over-spend or hoard.

What ever course they steer or chart
Has to start first with the heart,
So whatever cards life deals
The outcome can be one that heals.

Regardless of life's changing tide
Their one truth's carried deep inside—
It's more important to protect
Than it is to be correct.

New age thought they may deride;
They rely on what's been tried.
They come to know their god is near
Once they navigate through fear.

JUPITER IN LEO

Their viewpoints are impressive
And they clearly are expressive.
When they show us what they know
They really put on quite a show.
What they must guard against the most
Is their tendency to boast.

They're so confident and cheerful
And not likely to be fearful.
To act they don't need much detail,
They're so sure that they won't fail.
They won't do much second guessing
So you'll rarely find them stressing.

They're looked to for their leadership
Which can launch an ego trip.
They lead much better than they manage,
And they can spot and take advantage
Of opportunities or trends
They follow to successful ends.
They're excellent in how they coach
Us to do tasks that most won't broach.

An inner call, once they can hear it,
Navigates them to their spirit.
This quest of theirs becomes prodigious.
Some who try to be religious
May find church can't contain extremes.
They gravitate to larger themes.

JUPITER IN VIRGO

They're attracted to professions
Where they work in useful sessions
To bring perfection to details
On either small or larger scales.

They chase down all those little pieces
They expand to form their thesis.
The point in which they're really strong—
They're good at finding what went wrong
And then will work on how to fix it.
Rarely will they say to nix it.

They work hard when they are employed
Even if jobs aren't enjoyed.
At times they may accept too little,
Letting others chop and whittle
At ideals or worth they hold.
To grow through this they must be bold.

In learning to expand their borders
They grow best when not bound by orders,
But they must watch they're not derailed
By wanting to be too detailed.

Even though they're duty bound
They'll always show us beauty found.
Priests and priestesses of earth,
They find new ways of giving birth
To perfect beauty yet to be
Which in maturity they see.

JUPITER IN LIBRA

They can't help it, they seek fairness
And to that end promote awareness.
They explore life's outer edges,
Peeking through the fences, hedges,
Reporting so we understand
Just how our culture must expand
Our breadth of social ranges;
Then they work to make those changes.

Social order is their mirror
In which they see all patterns clearer.
Although it takes time to discern,
The point that they most need to learn
Is themes on which they fix attention
Are privately their points of tension.

Underneath they can get wild
Concerned life can't be reconciled.
Then they get depressed, can't bear it
If life provides no one to share it.

When they objectify perception
It can lead to self-deception.
They can't depend just on their mind.
They must reach in and work to find
That inner place where it's okay
To use just faith to feel their way.

JUPITER IN SCORPIO

While some may seek to grow through prayers,
They have to penetrate all layers.
Deep feelings and intensity
Propel them through all density
In which most others can get mired.
Resistance makes them more inspired.

Though they can make a million bucks,
Live in ease, all things deluxe,
They must exceed their comfort level
When face to face with each new devil.

Secrecy—they so enjoy it
And frequently they will employ it.
They have a holy reverence
For those who keep a confidence.

They're attracted to life's dramas
And to all the many traumas
They perceive to be the norm.
This gives them ways they can transform
Themselves and others, that's their gift—
Helping others sort and sift.

They only trust the higher power
They find within their darkest hour.

JUPITER IN SAGITTARIUS

They want to open up our minds
And introduce us to all kinds
Of thinking, wisdom of the ages,
Then introduce us to those sages.
They have a flame that's in them, burning,
To only seek truth for its learning.

Their philosophic diatribes
They'll punctuate with raucous jibes.
The thoughts they share will show insights
Their minds retrieved from mythic heights.
Though their expounding is astute
It's offered as an absolute,
So they can get hot and inflated
When they find themselves debated.

Preferring informality,
They live life in totality.
Since they regard their ethics highly
They won't often act too slyly.
They will overlook small flaws
As long as no one breaks the laws.

They're restless, must be on the move
And don't get stuck in some deep groove.
But with their focus pointed high
They might miss vital things close by.
Their minds are tuned to open wide
To seek the light that's found inside.

JUPITER IN CAPRICORN

Reality's their prime concern.
Among the first things that they learn
Is that planning and smart works
Are what bring life's many perqs.
They have a great ability
To take responsibility.

They like the trappings of prestige.
They understand noblesse oblige,
But not until they grow much older
Do they build up that strong shoulder
That lets people lean on them
Whom in youth they might condemn.

How they get some solid traction
Is to gear up, get in action.
They worry and don't feel complete
'Til plans take form, become concrete.
One danger that pulls them off track
Is if they concentrate on lack.
They seek the future through the past,
Old philosophies that last.
The spiritual for them must have

A solid base, not just be salve.
For them to grow, expand, they must
Exceed the practical they trust
And employ their intuition
Which they regard with some suspicion.

JUPITER IN AQUARIUS

Those in charge do not impress them.
In fact, they often will redress them.
They don't gladly suffer fools
And will push and stretch the rules.

For these folks it's not allowed
To be thought just one of the crowd.
They're rarely comfortable with norms.
They're always seeking new reforms.
Even if conservative
There comes a point where they must give
Consideration to new ways,
How best to enter each new phase.

They see the planet's needs as great.
They want to meet them now—why wait?
They work in groups to make life just;
It's one on one they don't quite trust.

Back up statements, have defense;
They'll make you give them evidence.
They first explore through mind, not heart.
They will often stand apart
Evaluating all they see.
That's how they find their deity.

JUPITER IN PISCES

They help in unassuming ways.
Their motivation isn't praise
But the value of good deeds
And helping others meet their needs.

Although they're pretty idealistic
They also can be fatalistic
And feel no matter what they do
They won't be able to live through
Those perils lying up ahead
That could leave them broke or dead.
Still somehow when they feel they're stuck
They're bailed out by a stroke of luck.

They're fairly tolerant of vices.
Their lives have many sacrifices
So they know of deep, deep sadness.
They see harmony and madness
Hand in hand in unity
In ways that few can truly see.

When life's waters get real muddy
They retreat alone to study.
Beliefs are lenses they see through,
Beliefs to which they will be true.
Don't tell them what they should believe.
You'll see their backs as they just leave.

CHAPTER 8
SATURN

There are no fun stories about Saturn. To briefly recap about him from the Jupiter chapter, his mother got him to kill his father, the brutal tyrant, Ouranos, king of the Titan First Gods. Continuing the story, just before he died, Ouranos prophesized that one of Saturn's own children would overthrow him, just as Saturn now did to him. In ancient life a prophecy was considered a *fait accompli*. Still, Saturn thought he could escape the prophecy's fulfillment by manipulating circumstances. He ordered his wife, Rhea, to immediately give him each child at birth whom he then devoured. By the time Jupiter came along his mother was desperate to have a living child so she conspired to have him hidden immediately after his birth. She wrapped a stone in infant's clothing telling Saturn it was their son. He quickly swallowed it, not noticing the deception. The prophecy was fulfilled—Jupiter did eventually overthrow him to become king of a new order of gods.

Saturn is best known as the god of time. His image most recognizable today is one we see each New Year. He is both the infant at the year's beginning and the bearded old man at year's end holding an hour glass and a sickle, symbolizing how time eventually runs out and cuts down all living things. Just as Saturn ate his children, so does he eat us all through the deteriorating effects of time on our mortal bodies. This doesn't place Saturn at the top of anyone's "most popular god" list.

In astrology Saturn is associated with restrictions and limitations, time being only one. He rules the maturation process of recognizing limitations and learning to overcome them. Unlike Jupiter through whom optimism and confidence flow, Saturn is usually first experienced as dread or fear. He has an austere effect on those not initiated in his ways, often first perceived as a club for ascetics no one wants to join. This is why the ancient astrologers referred to him as "the Greater Malefic." Yet as we age and reflect on our lives we see that he, our greatest disciplinarian, is also our greatest friend. Many of our successes come when we submit to his lessons. Likewise our failures come when we don't heed them or when we haven't yet developed the internal capacity to do so.

Saturn rules structures, from the bones that support our bodies to the governing and operating systems of business and government. He stands guard over all rules, laws, authorities, forms, discipline and enforcement until we are able to maintain them for ourselves. That is why Saturn's challenges appear to come from outside ourselves until we can finally understand why we attracted them in the first place or how we may have unknowingly contributed to them, like the opportunity we lost, the foreclosure on our house, the unraveling relationship, the annoyingly familiar overbearing boss we find at every job.

The lessons of Saturn involve changing only ourselves. No matter how hopelessly we seem imprisoned by the chains of outer conditions, our first task is to take responsibility for responding to our situation regardless of its cause. Unlike other planets, Saturn gives us a pretty dramatic "before and after" view of ourselves, the operation of time again. A good example of this is given in the film "The Natural." Toward the end of the film Glenn Close says to Robert Redford whose character is beating himself up for a past mistake, "I think we live two lives—the life we learn with and the life we live with after that."

Saturn is considered the "heavy" of the zodiac in contrast to Jupiter's good guy image, but that's deceiving. Behind the scenes father and son work perfectly together to keep us moving forward. Saturn's action is centripetal. It condenses and compresses energy into matter and form. Jupiter's energy is centrifugal, propelling us beyond our present limitations. The ancients knew this well as the original symbols for Saturn and Jupiter are identical, with one the inversion of the other. Jupiter imbues Saturn's forms and structures with the capacity for vision and relationship with what is beyond the material world. Likewise, Saturn gathers and condenses Jupiter's dreams and higher consciousness into forms that are life-sized and manageable for practical experience. So Saturn eats us, but with the expression of Jupiter's energy we are regurgitated out of our imprisonment and into new possibilities.

Following are examples of Saturn's and Jupiter's placement in one's chart to see how these opposing forces provide both challenges and opportunities, starting with a person who has Jupiter in flamboyant Leo and Saturn in analytical Virgo. Jupiter is casual about details and Jupiter in Leo is like throwing gasoline on a fire in that regard. As the verses reveal, the creative challenge is important, the call to leadership to inspire others, the love of being the center of attention. Virgo, on the other hand, practically burns incense at the altar of detailed analysis, so Saturn in Virgo provides an opposing inner need for structured analysis, paying attention to detail, getting things right, fixing what doesn't work, and to serve rather than to shine. Saturn in Virgo is offended by the mess the creations Jupiter in Leo can make. Jupiter in Leo likes to blow off Saturn in Virgo's demand that everyone paint within the lines. With this combination we can see the potential for internal conflict. However, the potential for success can be enormous when these two aspects of self acknowledge and learn from the other. This is a process that evolves over time and is accelerated by conscious attention to the gifts and lessons of each planetary expression.

Let's look at another example in which Jupiter is in conservative practical Taurus and Saturn is in Aquarius, the sign of the anarchist. Right away the verses reveal that Taurus isn't going to give Jupiter the free reign he has in Leo. Jupiter in Taurus expresses in a far more mundane and practical way. Goals are based on solid achievements that can be materially measured, actions completed along carefully plotted time lines, and all discussed over a good meal, of course. Surprisingly, practical Jupiter in Taurus has more of a friend in Saturn in Aquarius than one may first assume, since both placements require, as the verses indicate, substantial data and evidence to support their positions and actions along with measurements to evaluate them.

The potential for conflict comes not only in establishing goals but communicating them. Jupiter in Taurus will want a safe lucrative outcome and will be skilled in communicating how this will be done. Saturn in Aquarius will require that the outcome benefits humanity and brings something new into the world, and has a knack for structuring it in ways that people will accept. Saturn in Aquarius may not see much point in social niceties or smooth marketing plans and may be quite comfortable discussing business while standing around a street vendor's cart munching on a hot dog. The challenge for a person with these two placements is to find a way to integrate these known and safe territories with new ideas to create something innovative.

The noted psychoanalyst Carl Jung, when much closer to the end of his life than the beginning of it, described freedom as, "to gladly do the things I must," the intended result of our Saturn experiences. It is through our experiences of Saturn that we find freedom from situations we initially felt imprisoned by. There aren't many greater gifts in life than that.

Saturn is the farthest planet from the Sun covered in this book. It spends two and a half years in each sign and returns to its natal position roughly every 28½ years. These return periods constitute major markers in learning our particular individual and social responsibilities. Like Jupiter, Saturn is personal but also indicates our necessity to relate on a broader scale to the world we live in. Because of the length of time it spends in a sign, it is likely that the majority of your friends you grew up with share your Saturn sign. Therefore, characteristics of Saturn in each sign are not just personal but also characterize a subset of a generation.

The fastest and easiest way to find which astrological sign your Saturn is in is to search on the Internet for sites that calculate astrological charts for free. My Saturn is in the sign of _____.

SATURN IN ARIES

Their faces are masks that conceal
Deep feelings that they don't reveal.
They've obstacles in early years
That bring as many fears as tears.
They try to leave the past behind them
But it catches up to find them.

They're conflicted—should they act
Or not, afraid they'll be attacked.
They're singularly constituted
To expect to be refuted,

Thinking others will prohibit
Them and also try to limit
Freedom they so strongly seek.
In early years they can seem meek.
Throughout their lives they will be prone
To feel they work best when alone.
They must be careful that their need
For independence won't impede
Their give and take, the ways they share
With those for whom they really care.

Their lives get easier with age.
As they gain confidence they gauge
How they can balance independence
With a trusting safe dependence.

As they mature they learn to speak
And express how they're unique
And find ways that they can be free
To be who they so want to be.

SATURN IN TAURUS

These people look before they leap.
They need to feel that they can keep
What they have worked so hard to get.
They don't like to be in debt.
Though they have monetary need
They don't like other people's greed
And it makes them quite uneasy
When anyone is acting sleazy.

They make good use of what's at hand.
They're most at ease when things are planned
Since life has more complexities
Than make them truly feel at ease.

They must contemplate the cost
Of taking risks and getting lost.

That's how they learn they can trust life
Provides for them in times of strife.
There is no way that they'll be swayed
Once their goals and course are made.
At first they don't want to embrace
Changes they meet face to face,
But once they do some self-reflection
With depth that leads to introspection,
They can free themselves of fears
And find release in later years.

SATURN IN GEMINI

They start out rigid in their thinking
And they may have trouble linking
Facts when they learn something new.
They may not grasp it, have no clue
If what they're being taught lacks order
And isn't in some clear cut border.

When they search, investigate
It helps them learn to integrate
All information and discern
How to use the things they learn.
Then they get good at plotting courses
Using just their mind's resources.

Be sure that you get them involved
When there are problems to be solved.
Their remarkable expression
Of ideas will tend to freshen
All discussions and debates.
There's never too much on their plates.

If fear clouds their way with dread
They'll only see one step ahead,
But once they trust that step is there
There's little they won't try or dare.

SATURN IN CANCER

You may not have the slightest notion
Of their thinking or emotion.
It takes a while for them to show
Their thoughts and feelings, let you know,
Because they feel before they bond
They need to scope how you'll respond.

They need to understand their place
Within the family to erase
Unconscious patterns there concealed
That rule them 'til they are revealed.
Until that time they can make errors
In thinking that the source of terrors
Only comes from threats outside
Instead of something deep inside.

They need to do this on their own,
This work to find their comfort zone,
To rid themselves of inner fears
So they can in future years
Be the ones who calm the storm,
Have cool in crisis be their norm.

The values they will learn to treasure
Will have a very different measure
From the world, those based on caring
With the goal to increase sharing.

SATURN IN LEO

In youth they need to feel encouraged
Or else they can feel quite discouraged,
Then they become too self-reliant
And then they tend to be defiant.

They'll choose to work before they play.
They're good at using charm to sway

Others to their points of view
Or recruit them to their crew.

When they're in charge they will expect
That people work hard, show respect.
Their needs for recognition can
Cause well laid plans to hit the fan.
For them to do their very best
They have to pass an ego test.

Their search for meaning can collide
With their need to salvage pride.
With planning and with training,
Which at times they can find draining,
They build a new way to express
The loving heart that they possess.

They work the hardest for themselves.
Their gifts come forward when each delves
Deep inside their inner cores
Which will serve to open doors
Releasing creativity
Long held within captivity.

SATURN IN VIRGO

If they lack order when they're young
In later life they feel hamstrung
And tend to bog down in detail,
Then beat themselves up if they fail.

Throughout their lives they will deduce
Their worth by how they are of use.
They're strict on tasks, down to the letter,
They always want to do things better.
They're good at seeing things get done.
(Sometimes you want to get a gun.)

They're pleased with tasks precisely done
And battles that are nicely won.
Their demeanors show reserve.
They like to do tasks that will serve.

Health is one big indicator
Of their inner regulator.
Most of them will deify
Experiences that purify.
If in searching for perfection
They work at deeper introspection
And they don't like what they are seeing,
They'll reconstruct their inner being.

SATURN IN LIBRA

They use diplomacy and tact
In nearly every single act
Unless they think there's been a breach
Of fairness, then they lecture, preach.
When knowing what is right can stump us,
Check with them, our moral compass
To coolly work a problem through
To help us know just what to do.

Agreements are quite sacrosanct.
If you break them then you're tanked,
And those who do so lose their places,
Of top standing in good graces.

They won't be rushed into decision.
They've got to have time to envision
Every outcome, consequence.
Before they act it must make sense,
But while assessing each condition
They may ignore their intuition.

And they will chalk it up to fate
That once they've settled, picked a mate

They find that they are in a mess—
They've chosen what they can't express
Since their relationships portray
Their inner conflict, one which they
Must work inside to integrate it,
The only way they can abate it.

SATURN IN SCORPIO

With this placement of the stars
These people often carry scars
From a childhood battleground
On which they rarely will expound.

Possessions are how they keep score.
They know that under life there's more
But it is hard for them to dare
To open up and truly share.
What tops the list of things they fear
Is that they will disappear,
Resisting when faced with surrender,
Afraid that it will serve to render
Them as helpless, no control.
That's why they balk and then steamroll.

They must address their feeling states
Engaged in actions and debates
That are hidden by repression
And compulsive in expression.

Their strengths they find revealed in crisis,
Pealed back like the veils of Isis.
That's why they have to take the trouble
To sort through all their inner rubble
To learn to seek change, to explore
To be what they've not been before.
They come to understand that death
Is closely followed by new breath.

SATURN IN SAGITTARIUS

They take in information slowly.
They find the human mind quite holy.
They know meaning when they see it,
But their challenge? How to free it,
For they must work from inside out
To try to navigate about
So they can access what they know
And carry with them, make it flow.

In youth they're subject to tight rules
In their churches, homes or schools
That can hamper quests for knowledge,
Like if or where they go to college.

Others' faiths will not apply
Nor do they serve to satisfy.
If forced it leads to their rebellions
When some of them are branded hellions.
The best way that they understand
Is to find things out first hand.
As they develop they get bolder,
But often not until they're older
Can they break through rigid norms
To fit their psyches for new forms
So they'll no longer moralize
But will become those who are wise.

SATURN IN CAPRICORN

Their father's roles were prominent,
And if they were too dominant
Then they might feel that their mistakes
Will mar success, deny them breaks.

They're sensitive to ridicule.
They never want to look the fool.
Their roads to find their roles in life

Move slowly, often filled with strife,
But they can handle lots of tension
Since they focus their attention
On those tasks that must be done,
Specific battles to be won.

As they grow they concentrate
On strengths, not weakness, and abate
Straying from the task at hand.
Hard work is what they understand.
They think it sinful if they shirk
Any element of work.
Their ambition and persistence
Help them overcome resistance.

In later years as they grow older,
That duty demon on their shoulder
Increases how they're able
To make conditions strong and stable.

SATURN IN AQUARIUS

A little short on social graces,
They don't like superficial places.
Their actions make them seem aloof.
Their scientific minds need proof.
They're often apprehensive
So they tend to be defensive.

Their friendships will be few but strong.
The way they try to get along
Is seeking some community
For intimacy, unity,
Not first aware that they're not feeding
The intimacy that they're needing.

At first it's hard, reduced to meekness,
To try to show off their uniqueness.
That which breaks their isolation

Are their acts of new creation,
Extraordinary new inventions
Taking them to new dimensions.

They're geared to work on global themes
And some do so to great extremes.
In youth they're very idealistic
And as they age, get realistic.
With age they learn they're most effective
Bringing change to the collective.

SATURN IN PISCES

In youth they're not sure they are able
To make their futures strong and stable.
Within their consciousness are wed
Confidence in hand with dread.
They need support so they'll accept
They're capable and quite adept.

They need to have their roles defined.
They're idealistically inclined.
The works they do are beneficial.
The means they use are sacrificial.
They are prone to much compliance
When they're faced with some defiance.
They put others' needs ahead
Of theirs, then wish they'd not instead.

Their material ambition
Goes at some point in remission.
The reality they must embrace
Is a subjective one—they face
And come to know there's something greater.
They find their own way to Creator.
When they do they've clearly found
There truly is no battleground.

EPILOGUE

STAR CATCHER

It tugged at her, that ancient call,
so she slipped from her barren bed
  where her sisters in black were asleep,
to that magical night to catch stars soon to fall.

She ran through the trees to the open space,
she flew over crests of the hills;
  with joy she embraced those fiery streaks,
their burning caresses, their kiss on her face.

All night long she danced with that Light,
wrapped in its numinous arms;
  her blood ran white and hot with its fire
that forever would kindle her soul in the night.

Her days were cold in those walls of stone,
sorting the dried and withered fruit,
  sifting dead ashes scorched by the Sun,
while her sisters knelt silently weeping alone.

But at night she bathed in those radiant beams;
her hands still covered with silvery dust
  stroked the burning kiss on her skin,
and wild she ran with the stars in her dreams.

Deborah Smith Parker

RECORD OF PLANETS AND SIGNS

Name _____

Date of birth _____

Sun _____

Moon_____

Mercury_____

Venus_____

Mars_____

Jupiter _____

Saturn _____

Name _____

Date of birth _____

Sun _____

Moon_____

Mercury_____

Venus_____

Mars_____

Jupiter _____

Saturn _____

Name _____

Date of birth _____

Sun _____

Moon_____

Mercury_____

Venus_____

Mars_____

Jupiter _____

Saturn _____

Name _____

Date of birth _____

Sun _____

Moon_____

Mercury_____

Venus_____

Mars_____

Jupiter _____

Saturn _____

Name _____

Date of birth _____

Sun _____

Moon_____

Mercury_____

Venus_____

Mars_____

Jupiter _____

Saturn _____

Name _____

Date of birth _____

Sun _____

Moon_____

Mercury_____

Venus_____

Mars_____

Jupiter _____

Saturn _____

RECORD OF PLANETS AND SIGNS

Name _____
Date of birth _____
Sun _____
Moon _____
Mercury _____
Venus _____
Mars _____
Jupiter _____
Saturn _____

Name _____
Date of birth _____
Sun _____
Moon _____
Mercury _____
Venus _____
Mars _____
Jupiter _____
Saturn _____

Name _____
Date of birth _____
Sun _____
Moon _____
Mercury _____
Venus _____
Mars _____
Jupiter _____
Saturn _____

Name _____
Date of birth _____
Sun _____
Moon _____
Mercury _____
Venus _____
Mars _____
Jupiter _____
Saturn _____

Name _____
Date of birth _____
Sun _____
Moon _____
Mercury _____
Venus _____
Mars _____
Jupiter _____
Saturn _____

Name _____
Date of birth _____
Sun _____
Moon _____
Mercury _____
Venus _____
Mars _____
Jupiter _____
Saturn _____

Record of Planets and Signs

Name _____
Date of birth _____
Sun _____
Moon _____
Mercury _____
Venus _____
Mars _____
Jupiter _____
Saturn _____

Name _____
Date of birth _____
Sun _____
Moon _____
Mercury _____
Venus _____
Mars _____
Jupiter _____
Saturn _____

Name _____
Date of birth _____
Sun _____
Moon _____
Mercury _____
Venus _____
Mars _____
Jupiter _____
Saturn _____

Name _____
Date of birth _____
Sun _____
Moon _____
Mercury _____
Venus _____
Mars _____
Jupiter _____
Saturn _____

Name _____
Date of birth _____
Sun _____
Moon _____
Mercury _____
Venus _____
Mars _____
Jupiter _____
Saturn _____

Name _____
Date of birth _____
Sun _____
Moon _____
Mercury _____
Venus _____
Mars _____
Jupiter _____
Saturn _____

RECORD OF PLANETS AND SIGNS

Name _____
Date of birth _____
Sun _____
Moon_____
Mercury_____
Venus_____
Mars_____
Jupiter _____
Saturn _____

Name _____
Date of birth _____
Sun _____
Moon_____
Mercury_____
Venus_____
Mars_____
Jupiter _____
Saturn _____

Name _____
Date of birth _____
Sun _____
Moon_____
Mercury_____
Venus_____
Mars_____
Jupiter _____
Saturn _____

Name _____
Date of birth _____
Sun _____
Moon_____
Mercury_____
Venus_____
Mars_____
Jupiter _____
Saturn _____

Name _____
Date of birth _____
Sun _____
Moon_____
Mercury_____
Venus_____
Mars_____
Jupiter _____
Saturn _____

Name _____
Date of birth _____
Sun _____
Moon_____
Mercury_____
Venus_____
Mars_____
Jupiter _____
Saturn _____